Praise for *Nourishing Resistance*

"This collection of essays offers invaluable frameworks and inspirational models on how to get food out of capitalist markets and into the hands and stomachs of all. They fiercely demonstrate how the harvesting, growing, preparing, cooking, sharing, and eating of food has shaped and reshaped our cultures, created the social conditions for conviviality, and helped to break the seclusion and alienation that racist, capitalist patriarchies organize. A must-read for all who dream of keeping practices of commoning alive."
—Silvia Federici, author of *Re-enchanting the World: Feminism and the Politics of the Commons*

"A thoughtfully assembled, refreshingly global collection of radical voices who urge us to reimagine the meaning of the phrase 'food is political.'"
—Mayukh Sen, author of *Taste Makers: Seven Immigrant Women Who Revolutionized Food in America*

"Prepare to be nourished by this book. In these essays, contributors share personal and collective stories of grassroots food activism from around the world. From community kitchens to queer potlucks to critical analyses of public space, diet culture, and property—you'll witness how they reimagine food beyond the food-enterprise status quo. Each essay is intimate. As the authors revisit what community, sovereignty, radical, and other concepts mean, they address concepts that are often taken for granted in food-related activism and scholarship. While lifting up the significance of food in social movements, they make fresh connections between movements whose stories are often told separately. There are no prescriptive 'solutions' here, thank goodness. This collection is a reminder that kitchen-sink food activism is taking place everywhere and is happening now. By sharing their stories, the authors invite us to reconsider our commitments, our assumptions, and what we think is possible."
—Naya Jones, assistant professor, University of California Santa Cruz

T0054448

"This beautiful and thought-provoking collection of essays brings together reflections on the role of food in Indigenous land defense, immigrant ritual, international social centers, queer belonging, and so much more. I finished the book reinvigorated to bring radical attention to the ways in which our meals truly make our movements. *Nourishing Resistance* reminds us that any project toward liberation has a common root: the need for nourishment."
—Raechel Anne Jolie, author of *Rust Belt Femme*

"This book is delicious in all seven colors of the rainbow, as we say in South Africa about a balanced meal that is diversely nutritious. It is the queer potluck club where new friends bring casseroles of dangerously loving inscriptions of a future that is free and freeing. It is a buffet of radical imaginations of past, present, and future cooperatives fighting for new arrangements of society that facilitate self-determination, intersectional justice, and equity. This meditation and manifesto on food brings into focus how food—its presence, its cultures, its systems, and its work—is vital to any liberatory or emancipatory agenda. Food is not only essential for cultivating multigenerational connection and community outside of the nuclear family structure, as one writer notes, but also for prying apart all sorts of binaries to release new possibilities and futures. When you are done, lick your fingers. They will taste like canned beans left along migrant trails in Arizona, homemade sourdough that stood up against coal giants, and the stew that was a tool to foster closer bonds in the migrant residents of Constitución. There will be nothing to waste."
—Kneo Mokgopa, writer and artist

"Reading *Nourishing Resistance* fills me with a feeling of possibility and a renewed appreciation for the transformative power that exists in the simple act of sharing food with those around you. This collection of essays shifts the paradigm away from the binary of frontlines work and support work and toward a view of movement building that sees everyone's contributions as absolutely essential to the health and viability of the whole movement—from scrubbing dishes to creating a blockade, from jail support to boiling rice. To me, there's nothing more empowering than seeing tangible examples of people using their gifts to cook up unique and life-giving contributions to the social movements around them, and this collection is full of those."
—Ciro Carrillo, *Mutual Aid on Lockdown* podcast

"Like a song that makes you feel like you can take on the world, this collection of interviews, poetry, essays, and story is a chorus of activists, academics, artists, farmers, writers, sex workers, teachers, and other disruptors, whose writings teach, inspire, and challenge in offering new visions for what can be when we act on aspirations for a world in which every person's right to food, love, and dignity are taken for granted. The many notes include historical and contemporary pieces on topics that range from radical farming and food sovereignty, the solemnity and pleasure of eating and feeding, fat activism and emerging unapologetically from the margins, immigration and the politics of care, capitalism, and revolution to celebrating queer joy. Each voice puts a finger on the deep personal and shared relationships we have with food and shows how those can be put in service of creating collective commitments that better sustain our hearts, minds, and hands in connection with the land that gives us life."
—Dr. Jennifer Brady, registered dietitian and director of the School of Nutrition and Dietetics at Acadia University in Mtaban/ Wolfville, Mi'kma'ki/Nova Scotia, Turtle Island/Canada

"The collection of rich stories, analytic accounts, and thought-provoking interviews in this book is a wonderful read for anyone curious about or working toward liberatory food cultures today. These activist-writers take us through inspiring and intriguing examples of food as mutual aid, food in practices of decolonization, and food as deeply embedded with rebellion. A beautiful and provocative set of pieces that whet the appetite for cooking up revolution and care."
—Michelle Glowa, assistant professor in the Anthropology and Social Change Department at the California Institute of Integral Studies

"*Nourishing Resistance* transports us from the coalfields of West Virginia to farmer protests in India and far beyond, reminding us of the global role of food and collectivism in the fight against oppression and injustice. A truly humanizing and nourishing anthology that reminds us of the inherent politics and power of food."
—Debbie Weingarten, journalist

Nourishing Resistance

Stories of Food, Protest, and Mutual Aid

Edited by Wren Awry

Nourishing Resistance: Stories of Food, Protest, and Mutual Aid
© Wren Awry
This edition © PM Press 2023

ISBN: 978-1-62963-992-5 (paperback)
ISBN: 978-1-62963-996-3 (ebook)
Library of Congress Control Number: 2022943234

Cover by John Yates / www.stealworks.com
Interior design by briandesign

10 9 8 7 6 5 4 3 2 1

PM Press
PO Box 23912
Oakland, CA 94623
www.pmpress.org

Printed in the USA.

Contents

Foreword

Cindy Barukh Milstein

It might seem paradoxical for someone who can't cook to write a fore-word for a collection of pieces—a hearty stew, as it were—about food.

I used to dread, for instance, as I suspect my housemates did too, when it was my turn to make dinner for an anarchist collective of some twenty people. I'm also *that* person at potlucks who brings an uninspired store-bought item, sneaking it onto the table out of embarrassment when no one's looking, rather than a home-baked delight like a yummy vegan casserole with ingredients from one's own garden or a scrumptious seven-layer cake decorated with foraged edible flowers. And even when Wren, during the chilly days of the pandemic, warmly snail-mailed me their "foolproof" recipe for antifascist eggplant parm, handwritten on a note-card, the result of my kitchen labors was a gloppy, unappetizing mess.

Yet as I read through the stories in *Nourishing Resistance*, I realized that food, as rebelliously understood in this anthology, has little to do with whether one has culinary skills or not.

It's enough, say, to immerse one's hands in soapy water and be *that* person, aka me, who gladly does the dishes or leaps into setup and cleanup for big communal gatherings. It's enough to scavenge for salvaged food-stuffs as part of a mutual aid project, or ladle out entrées at an outdoor Food Against Fascism share or pipeline encampment lunch, or leave jugs of water and cans of beans in the desert borderlands as gestures of hospitality as well as solidarity for undocumented travelers, or concoct the prefigurative spaces of collective care, autonomous community, and intimate connections that happen when we include the simple act of "breaking bread" together. It's enough to recognize that food is not only life; it is one of the key ingredients in us cooking up lives worth living.

As my own lack of cooking skills attests to, though, having various ingredients on hand doesn't necessarily add up to a nourishing repast.

What this delectable blend of essays showed me, perhaps as the first step in any sort of recipe for liberatory transformation, is that we need to remember what food has been and what it could and should be again—and in some cracks and crevices of possibility, still is. Centuries of battles and, alas, defeats over sustenance have, in myriad ways, stolen so much from us, distancing us from the very notion that we can indeed directly determine and cooperatively provide what we all need to thrive. It's not only that colonizers were thieves of all sorts of Indigenous wisdom, down to the smallest seeds, and that capitalist thieves killed off the commons with fences and borders. They and other representatives of deadly regimes robbed food of its abundant meanings, from contexts and varieties to cultures and interrelationships. Food became homogenized into a global commodity and thus a means of wealth accumulation, social control, and geopolitics for an insatiable few.

Time and again, millions of our ancestors put up a fight in defense of their diet, which for millennia meant not some narrow, judgmental restriction of food but rather, as in the ancient Greek *diaita*, an expansive "way of living." This book aids us in remembering that food has played an essential part in, as the ancient Greek *diaitasthai* signaled, how to "lead one's life," or what might be understood as self-governing one's life with others. Indeed, we will only be able to fully inhabit life if we routinely assemble (an archaic definition of the word *diet*) to self-determine "sacred and shared space," as contributor Cheshire Li puts it, "working together to create… delicious and magical" social as well as ecological relations. We see this crucial role of food in everything from riots, uprisings, and outright revolutions to joyous and life-giving as well as life-honoring festivals and rituals, from neighborhood gatherings and grassroots political organizing to the humble, everyday "excuse" to circle around a table or crowd a kitchen in our desire to sustain ourselves and the processes of life.

This anthology isn't the first time that Wren has generatively provoked my own remembrances of the power of food and its place in the most meaningful of moments—when all feels as it should. I initially met Wren after a mutual writerly pal connected us when I was in search of poetic, poignant, messy-beautiful prose for an edited volume on the collective work of grief. Wren became a contributor and, I'm grateful to say, a friend now too. Their piece in *Rebellious Mourning* demonstrated how much food can be a holder of particularly impactful experiences—times and places in which we've loved and lost so much, thereby (re)affirming our dedication to mending the world. In this case, it was Wren's participation in resistance and grieving in Appalachia while fighting mountaintop removal side by side with local residents:

> What I recall best are details of my life in southern West Virginia, the things I saw and experienced on a day-to-day basis.... I remember eating hunted venison—rich and earthy, cooked into stroganoff, or sautéed up with garlic and onions—in fall, and sharp ramp onions in April. I recall, too, some of the practical knowledge I accrued ... [like] the proper way to make cowboy coffee (pour in two cups of cold water and tap the pot with a metal spoon to sink the grounds).[1]

Yet Wren doesn't just write about food; they weave it into the whole of life, past, present, and future. In fact, they view it, and embody it, as inseparable from how we could and should journey well through life and death, side by side with our ancestors and those who will come after us.

I joined in one example of that firsthand during a long, luxurious, vulnerably tender "workshop" of collective grieving, hosted on Shabbat by the Jewish History Museum, partly housed in a former synagogue in Tucson, Arizona, and facilitated by myself and three contributors to the *Rebellious Mourning* collection, including Wren. The room was already full of ghosts, so many displaced from these or other lands due to everything from colonialism and capitalism to anti-Semitism and racism and much more. As we Jews say, though, "May their memory be a blessing," or, for us anarchistic Jews, "May their memory spark a blessed revolution." So the four of us, not all Jews, shaped the Friday evening to allow those of us gathering to not only remember profound losses but also re-*member* our broken selves by drawing strength from all of our senses, and hence be better able to re-*member* this broken world. Our sacred time-space together included everything from a Shabbes ritual—with egg-based, vegan, and gluten-free homemade challah, along with the light of candles, taste of wine or juice, sound of blessing, and, as we broke off pieces of the bread, gently intertwined touch, like the braids in the loaves—to voicing stories, writing down reflections, and creating a collective altar.

For that temporary, do-it-ourselves altar, Wren contributed "the tradition of funeral biscuits," baking nettle and honey shortbread in enough abundance that we all got to eat one. Wren explained their deep interest "in the way recipes are used to honor the dead"—and, I would add, can somatically aid us in integrating such losses to make them bearable, without ever forgetting the love those losses will always represent, so as to feel whole. In describing the contribution afterward, Wren noted:

> I added honey to them because in many cultures around the world, the dead were and are buried or honored with honey. Then I thought about nettle. Nettle, which is often considered a weed and derided for its stinging hairs, grows on disturbed ground and in the foundations of abandoned buildings. It flourishes in those "waste places," providing an incredible array of health benefits and nutrients to those who harvest and use it as food and/or medicine. The herb felt like an apt metaphor for many of my radical, anarchist, feminist, and queer teachers and ancestors, all of whom came from rocky lives and unstable ground, but tirelessly strove for collective liberation and to build a new world in the shell of the old.[2]

Wren, of course, isn't alone in recognizing that food nourishes us through all of life's seasons and cycles, nor in practicing ways that food binds us to each other and the nonhuman world, nor in understanding that food is always already political, and it's how we engage in that "politics" that matters. As we've seen the past few years, for instance, powerful social movements, most keenly including self-organized communities of direct action and collective care, have coalesced around what should be self-evident to all humans, such as the lived ethics of "water is life." This anthology's contributors supply us, their reader-guests, with a banquet of sustenance—much needed at a time when we're starved for a sense of well-being and utopian futurity, given that the very survival of our species is in question.

Certainly, at this existential and palpable crossroads in human history, there are no guarantees of surviving, much less thriving. Yet there never were any such assurances. As this collection underscores, the only "recipe" that has ever worked over thousands of years is when we have daily dined, figuratively and literally, on reciprocal relationships to each other and the earth, on dignified and egalitarian lives in common, on the inherent worth of all life. When we knew, just as we know that we need to refuel our bodies every day in order to live, that "we are all we have," and moreover, "we are all we need," as contemporary mutual aid efforts often assert. Or, as contributor Alyshia Gálvez articulates it, "When we share, we are replenished."

What stuck to my ribs after finishing the last page of this volume was my own sense of replenishment. While reading this book, I remembered innumerable otherworldly moments in my own life when food had not only, as Lindsey Danis portrays in her essay about queer potlucks, been integral to the cultivation of communal "spaces for multigenerational connection outside of the nuclear family structure," but had also been perfect for prying apart all sorts of other binaries and boxes, thereby gifting so many potentialities. Whenever food filled a critical role in small or large collectivities, it cracked open space for simultaneously "rehearsing for rebellion" and "remaking the commons," to borrow the titles of, respectively, Alessandra Bergamin's piece and the contribution by Gaye Chan and Nandita Sharma.

For example, I recalled not my agony at having to cook dinner for those twenty-plus anarchist housemates of mine mentioned above. Instead, I was flooded with precious memories of us inventing the idea of Coffee Not Cops—probably around our big, boisterous, queered commons of a kitchen table—to both resist the implementation of a 24-7 police presence on a "ground zero" plaza in San Francisco's gentrification class-war zone *and* carve out a free and autonomous social gathering spot for all who were considered displaceable or even disposable. Over the months, it grew into a neighborhood hub, including everything from free pastries (not police), free cups of coffee (not cops), and free literature to freely shared gossip along with eviction defense advice and actions, from honoring Alex Nieto, murdered by cops mere blocks away, to folks self-organizing live music, dancing, art making, and other fun and festivities—and so much more, re-*membering* so many fractured parts of this community.

Savor this anthology, and while you do, chew on your own remembrances of when food, in its biggest, wildest, most fantastic senses, made you and many others around you feel fully who you could and should be. Then imagine forward. And start cooking up your own ways, practices, wisdoms, spaces, cultures, languages, times, delights, interventions, inspirations, rituals, and on and on, of how food can and should be life.

Or perhaps more pointedly, speaking to the collective trauma that this current social order is dishing up, I hope that *Nourishing Resistance* reminds you of why—whether you prefer to sauté veggies or scour the resulting saucepans—food, expansively envisioned, is so essential for any sort of dreamy social transformation and, as Wren phrased it to me, kitchen-sink solidarity. "We know time doesn't heal all wounds," contributor sumi dutta maintains, "but food just might help us metabolize them."

Cindy Barukh Milstein
Montreal, August 2021

Notes

1   Wren Awry, "Lungful of Mountain," in *Rebellious Mourning: The Collective Work of Grief*, ed. Cindy Milstein (Chico, CA: AK Press, 2017), 108.

2   Wren Awry, "Nettle and Honey Shortbread for Collective Mourning (and a Writing Exercise)," *Wren Awry Writes* (blog), January 20, 2020, https://wrenawrywrites. wordpress.com/2020/01/20/nettle-honey-shortbread-for-collective-mourning-a-writing-exercise/.

Introduction

Wren Awry

"Is there a food or meal that transports you to a memory of organizing, resistance, or mutual aid?" I asked on social media four or five years ago. I didn't expect to get many responses. As someone who was introduced to food-based solidarity through Food Not Bombs, helped cook breakfast in an environmental direct action campaign, and worked many long nights as a dishwasher and line cook, I'd long thought about the role food played in my life and the projects I was part of. But I also noticed that food was something the communities I belonged to didn't talk about much. If anything, the reproductive labor of cooking and cleaning up afterward was considered a thankless job, necessary but not nearly as important as strategizing for a street protest, documenting a lockdown, or providing first aid after a large-scale disaster.

When I checked back a few hours later, I was surprised. More than a dozen friends had responded, and some were having full-fledged conversations with one another in the comments. Stories poured in about green curry at Occupy Wall Street, ready-to-eat meals that provided sustenance to grassroots first responders after Hurricane Katrina, and hot cocoa handed out at a teachers' union blockade in Oaxaca. One commenter recalled the solidarity cultivated through passing out pastries to people as they were released from jail, while another remembered the jar of peanut butter that served as a favorite treat throughout a long tree sit. A few friends even casually theorized about why food work matters, asserting that it's an act of care and a way to pool resources and build community resilience.

Inspired by that conversation, I started interviewing people for a series called Nourishing Resistance, hosted by the now-defunct food blog *Bone + All*. I spoke with disaster relief cooks, food justice organizers, community gardeners, food studies scholars, and many others. The interviewees talked about cooking soup in parking garages to avoid police surveillance and working with high schoolers to map community food resources, including container gardens and generationally important dishes. They shared favorite recipes for mole, masoor daal, and high-volume potato salad. Each conversation left me excited for the next, and the series became a way to share those dialogues with others and carve out a bit of space to talk about the part food plays within anticapitalist and antiauthoritarian movements.

Then the opportunity arose to edit this anthology. As daunting as it seemed (yes, I'm still amazed that I had the chance to edit this book and hope that I did it with enough care and love), it also felt like a way to hold space for an even greater number of radical food stories. After putting out a call for pitches as well as contacting folks who I knew were already thinking and writing about food, I spent three years working through drafts with and learning from a wide range of contributors. This book, *Nourishing Resistance*, named after the original interview series, is the result.

This anthology goes far beyond what I could ever have imagined, with writing on everything from toxic diet culture to food packaging and disability to farming as a practice of liberation and resilience. A few of the original Nourishing Resistance interviews are included, while other interviewees have contributed new work, including a piece on the lessons learned—about gardening, cooking, and confronting capitalism—from a beloved great-grandmother as well as an essay on the wine industry's entrenchment in capitalism and colonialism. One article shares how Anishinabeg communities have organized to defend their land and the moose on it from settler sport hunters, while other contributors chronicle the communal kitchens that have been or are part of the Shaheen Bagh movement in Delhi, Movimiento Popular Nuestramérica in Buenos Aires, and anticapitalist organizing in Hong Kong. While some writers look to the past—from the gender dynamics of communes in the US West to anticolonial resistance in India—others imagine liberatory food futures in bold and delicious ways. And because many of these pieces were written during the ongoing pandemic, COVID-19's impacts on food security and community building crop up throughout these pages, from food-based mutual aid in the Bronx to the creative ways queer communities have used meals to sustain connectivity in times of social distancing. The authors, who write from a range of perspectives, don't always agree, and time and again I've found that their work both challenges and edifies my thinking on various food-related issues.

Nourishing Resistance is, of course, just one small part of a growing constellation of conversations, projects, and publications dedicated to sharing stories about food, protest, and mutual aid. It's intended as a book of narratives—personal, political, speculative, and all of the above— that aim to add to our collective understanding of the role food plays in liberatory politics and popular struggle. If you're new to the themes in this volume, I invite you to look for the places in your own life where food-based mutual aid and solidarity already exists, or where they could flourish, and consider getting involved with projects in your own communities, from weeding a collective garden to washing a round of dishes at a protest encampment to delivering groceries for an autonomous food distribution network. If you're already engaged in food-based organizing and community work, I hope you'll find the thinking, reporting, and remembering in *Nourishing Resistance* as fortifying and thought-provoking as I have. May it inspire you to continue this work and, if you wish, share your own stories of food and resistance with others.

On Feeding Others as an Act of Resistance

an interview with Cheshire Li

Cheshire Li has cooked for several disaster relief efforts and direct actions since they hopped on the Everybody's Kitchen bus, a traveling activist kitchen, in 2009. Since then, they've prepared food for anti-mountaintop-removal campaigns in West Virginia, for the Tar Sands Blockade in Texas, in solidarity with land defenders on Black Mesa, and for relief efforts for Hurricane Sandy, Hurricane Harvey, and Hurricane Michael. In addition to their culinary talents, Cheshire is an artist and storyteller who turns recipe notes into commentary on state repression and finds the poetry in everyday acts of solidarity.

Since this interview was originally published in spring 2018, Cheshire has set up a home base in Denver and has dipped into the logistics side of activist kitchen work, including coordinating shipping and receiving, inventory, conflict mediation, large equipment, finances, and other moving pieces for the Family of Friends Relief Effort in response to Hurricane Michael. They also work as a pedicab operator and spend time mountain biking, snowboarding, traveling, and cooking for themselves and others: they recently filled an entire Moleskine notebook with recipes they've collected through the pandemic and made "literal gallons of chili oil" to send to friends across the country. Cheshire is also deeply invested in diverse film work that centers people of color and queer folks, as well as intersecting photography and film with their love of cycling and the outdoors. They freelance in film as a grip and assistant camera and pursue freelance photo work in the outdoors. Their current short documentary project centers women and queer people of color on mountain bikes and features a cast and crew that is composed entirely of queer, trans, and femme members. Cheshire believes that centering stories at the most vulnerable intersections of our communities is key to creating and holding spaces where we can learn to thrive together.

When did you start cooking? What is it about food that draws you in?
When you ask, "When did you start cooking?" the question that I actually hear is, "When did you get on the kitchen bus?" In my mind, that was the beginning of my hunger: a hunger for community, for a more equitable world, for a diversity of experience in my life, for deeply fulfilling work that I could do with my hands. That hunger was when I began to view and understand food through a radical lens.

I grew up surrounded by traditional Chinese food, and by cooks: my grandfather, my great-aunt and great-uncle, and my cousin all owned and managed Chinese restaurants. My grandfather was the first in my family to emigrate here to the States, and it was a really common practice for Chinese immigrants (and many other people of color, displaced from the familiar flavors of their homelands and cuisines) to open restaurants and to continue making and sharing the food and culture they were suddenly severed from in a new country. They did everything—they were the chefs, the servers, the line cooks and dishwashers—and they started from almost nothing and worked really hard for what they had. It was a way to survive, a way to hold on to a culture through familiar tastes and familiar movements in cooking.

Somewhere in my teenage years, though, I grew disillusioned with the strictness of the culture I was born from, and I didn't get along with my parents, so I didn't really start learning how to cook traditional Chinese food till later, and I still have a lot to learn.

I was so lucky to run into Everybody's Kitchen (EK) very early on in my travels. I should offer some explanation about this mean, orange, capitalism-killing machine called Everybody's Kitchen here: it's a kitchen project that's been active for about twenty-five years; the current itera-tion resides in a thirty-eight-foot school bus by the endearing name of Clementine, which includes a solar panel and battery bank setup, three-piece industrial deep sink, two stainless steel counters, speed racks, a six-burner Vulcan propane stove with two ovens and a flat top, a motley assortment of industrial pots (the largest of which I can climb inside), a roof rack welded out of old combine parts, and enough dry goods to survive the apocalypse or, better yet, the revolution.

Everybody's Kitchen was born and built from the vision of a hand-ful of scrappy itinerants, hippies, and punks over twenty-five years ago. Seated in beliefs of anticapitalism, a disillusionment with the state and its authority, consensus-based decision making, and the adamant conviction that healthy food is a fundamental human right and therefore should be free, the kitchen is an autonomous, grassroots, donation-funded project determined to help build a more equitable and less hungry world. The crew is composed of a loosely organized, rotating cast who travels the States and offers free food support to homeless encampments, inner city neighborhoods, activist camps, and counterprotests. Anybody is welcome to eat with us or to cook with us.

I met Anne and Victor, two staples of EK's core crew, at the Rainbow Gathering in New Mexico in 2009; I had just hit the road for the first time and I was twenty and really pretty naive, not yet radicalized, but when my friend Vanish put out a call to action later that year and asked me to come and cook with the bus in Pittsburgh for the G20 protests, I went without reservations. That's the first time I really worked with the bus.

I spent most of my time prepping vegetables by the hundreds of pounds, and we all spent a fair amount of time being moved about and harassed by the cops. We were forcibly relocated three times, from an art warehouse to a vacant school lot and finally a church parking lot, where the pastor put his foot down and said, "Well, if they want to arrest you, they'll have to arrest me too." The city really targeted us, along with the medics and the media, because we were providing the bulk of food support for counterprotesters. During all this chaos, harassment, and sleeplessness, I'm proud to say we never missed putting out a single meal. In Pittsburgh, I learned that food was critical and powerful and that food could be revolutionary; in fact, sharing food could be so radical that we were threatened with arrest and police violence, and simply persisting in sharing food in the face of repression was a really radical act.

In a wider lens, food draws me in very simply because I find a beauty in cooking and always have; baking in particular has always been special. Cooking is like this alchemy for me: control of heat, of ratios, understanding processes and chemistries, intuiting tastes, how they pair and work together, balance each other out. I love working with my hands, and the kitchen is traditionally such a sacred and shared space where everyone convenes—a space inherently based in community, in working together to create something delicious and magical. It's as much about the process as the end result; the creation is as important as the breaking of bread. I've always used food as a way to share myself with others, and when I think of cooking, that idea is inseparable from who I'll be making that food with and who I'll be eating it with. It's such a simple, soulful way to nourish others, to feed our bodies and minds and spirits with meaningful community, thoughtful work, and the shared fruits of our labors.

You've cooked for disaster relief efforts and protest campaigns. Could you talk a little bit about those experiences? What do you think are the connections between activism, mutual aid, and cooking?

My experience cooking with social/environmental justice campaigns has been so varied and diverse: I've grilled venison at Mountain Justice Summer in West Virginia, made mutton stew and fry bread on Black Mesa, conned the local grocery store out of compost for imaginary chickens for the Tar Sands Blockade in Texas, and baked homemade sourdough with a culture I carried from Texas to St. Louis for a summit against Peabody Coal. I've also carried gallons of water and cans of beans to leave along migrant trails in Arizona, helped manage a kitchen putting out over a thousand meals a day post–storm surge after Hurricane Sandy in New Jersey, and worked in a disaster relief kitchen serving a predominantly Latinx community after the flooding from Hurricane Harvey in Houston, Texas.

I feel like all of these experiences are so different and incomparable, although two strings tie them together in my mind: there was a need for food, and that need was filled by a radical grassroots group. Most of my experience in sharing food has been in grassroots kitchens, and I think that experience has really shown me what's possible in the realm of mutual aid, radical food, and food as activism.

In a capitalist, colonialist, racist culture and economy where access to food, healthy options, and food education are monetized and highly intersectional with race and class, sharing food becomes, suddenly, an intrinsically radical act. Floppy, one of the founders of Everybody's Kitchen, would say that no matter where we were or who we were serving, anybody who was hungry and wanted food would never be turned away. Regardless of race, class, appearance, social status, or any other factor, our goal was to share healthy, home-cooked, free food with anyone who was hungry without judgment—even if they were rich, even if they were a cop (and trust me, Floppy really hates cops). Hunger is such a universal feeling, and while we focused on serving homeless communities, activist camps, and low-income neighborhoods of color, the need for food transcends all of these divisions. In this way, food felt like something we could use as a healing force, and hunger felt like a feeling that could unite diverse communities.

In a culture where people are trained to pay for everything, to monetize any and all transactions, giving something as simple as food away becomes a paradigm shift for everyone involved—food becomes a gift that's quite arguably more difficult to receive than to give. By sharing food, Everybody's Kitchen aimed to shatter the dominant paradigm that assigns meaning and self-worth to race, class, ableism, gender, or sexuality, to destroy the idea that dignity and respect (and a right to healthy food) are earned through hard work and by overcoming obstacles in a world that's inequitable. We firmly believe that dignity and respect are inherent in all of us and that food is, and always will be, a fundamental human right.

On Everybody's Kitchen, our motto has always been "Solidarity Not Charity." This meant that we didn't come with the intention of being charitable, and we didn't want to be a group of outsiders serving people that we felt needed our help. Our goal was to connect with and be a part of the communities that we served food to and cooked with, to share our skill sets, and, ideally, to leave a community-run kitchen behind when we moved on. One of the most humbling things I learned when working with communities in places that had seen ecological and social injustice, disaster, or struggle at the hands of systems of oppression was to listen, first and foremost, and to earn trust and respect by acting with trust and respect. For me, mutual aid is inextricably tied to the practices of radical food share and support: as equals, within a consensus-based decision-making structure, prioritizing local leadership, and hearing and honoring local needs.

The practice of making and sharing food together feels like such a real and honest process in which I've learned to set boundaries and work with so many diverse people, to bring my own struggles to the table and understand how I fit into so many different communities, and to respect where others are and meet them. It's humbling, and so illuminating, to say the least.

What is the most interesting kitchen-related situation you've found yourself in?
There are so many stories that I could tell you about all the adventures that food justice has led me to... it's hard to choose, really. When I think of mutual aid and the controlled chaos that epitomizes disaster relief, I always think of the kitchen that we set up after Hurricane Sandy in New Jersey. It was one of the wildest kitchens I've ever been a part of: it was the

first time I'd helped manage a kitchen crew of probably eighty or more people, and the first time I'd worked disaster relief. I arrived within a week after Hurricane Sandy made landfall there, and the New Jersey coastline was absolutely wrecked. There was a *Time* magazine cover that came out later that year with that iconic yellow two-story house with two-thirds missing, and the roof was somehow still intact, perched on top of this sliver of house. That was in Union Beach, New Jersey, where we were.

Early organizers, many of them from the core crew of Everybody's Kitchen and other peripheral kitchens, had scouted and set up at a firehouse in town. We had water, miraculously, but no power; the entire neighborhood was running on generators. Everyone started putting out calls to action and gathering kitchen gear and a crew. People came from California, Montana, Michigan, Wisconsin, Texas, Louisiana, North Carolina, New York, Arizona—we came from literally every corner of the country. Core organizers were in touch with the incident command system at the county and state levels, but the magic of this kitchen was that while we were talking to and working around these power structures (that commonly direct many large nonprofit disaster response teams, the Red Cross being the iconic example), we were not funded by them, and we were therefore autonomous from their demands. Our funding came partially from Organic Valley, who also graciously donated so much equipment and kitchen gear, but for the most part, we were kept afloat by small donations from friends, family, and strangers.

The Union Beach Firehouse Grill, as we came to be called, began in two ten-by-ten-foot army tents with several crab cookers and a motley assortment of industrial kitchen gear cobbled together from the Rainbow Gathering kitchens closest to us in Asheville and upstate New York. It was snowing when I arrived, there was a core crew of perhaps a dozen people there, and the kitchen was still being built. From here, we knocked out the essentials: we tested our water; someone wrangled a port-a-potty donation; Navigator got us diesel and propane donations to keep the generator and stoves running; Amazing Dave handled site security; Baker Bob convinced the county to send us a fifty-three-inch refrigeration unit.

It's really hard for me to describe just how inspiring and wonderful this kitchen was, to encompass the feeling of momentum and unity it brought. New gear and fresh faces rolled in every day, and within a week and a half, the army tents had turned into food storage and we had expanded to fill out a canopy tent, replete with a row of at least eight crab cookers, an arsenal of sixty to eighty quart pots, two or three rows of prep tables, two three-piece industrial deep sinks for dishes, and propane heaters that we would huddle around on the cold nights. The yard of the firehouse was filled with tents where volunteers camped, and as word got out about the kitchen, friends and strangers got in touch and flew, drove, and bused in from all over to volunteer.

People from all walks of life passed through for hot meals: volunteer construction crews that had come in from surrounding states to help gut houses, people living in the surrounding communities who didn't have power, heat, or water. A FEMA crew came through and remarked that we had served them the best meal they'd had in the field; the Red Cross began to drop off Cambro containers of food on our line. Neighbors from less affected surrounding communities came and offered whatever they could give: massages, manicures, haircuts, food, equipment. A local restaurant owner came and asked us to name a piece of industrial kitchen equipment we needed but did not have, and he returned the next day with an industrial immersion blender, which was promptly put to use on a creamy curried cashew-coconut-sweet-potato soup.

At the culmination of this wild, chaotic, incredible kitchen, we served over 1,200 meals a day and sent out two satellite functions: the U-Hungry Cafe used a donated U-Haul truck to shuttle food to housebound neighbors and to hotels where storm victims were living, and Richard handed out hot grilled-cheese sandwiches from an Organic Valley kitchen van. On a typical day, most of us worked up to twenty hours, there were up to a hundred volunteers in the kitchen, we prepped vegetables by the hundred-pound case and made coffee ten gallons at a time, and the next meal was always on the stove. Donations showed up by the truckload, and Alice set up and managed a distribution center for clothing, food, and household goods. Someone donated a bounce house for the kids, Diamond Dave started an open mic, and the kitchen exploded into a full-blown block party with a row of grills and smokers outside the dining area.

At some point, someone in the incident command system offered the kitchen a large amount of funding if we would relocate to a different location, and Bob came to the core crew to get a consensus decision on the proposal. We basically unanimously agreed that the new location wasn't where we wanted to be and that the community we had chosen to set up in had a greater need, and we turned the money down. That was a really powerful feeling, that we had built from scratch this miraculous, community-centered kitchen and that we could make autonomous decisions about where we wanted to be and how we wanted to run things. And that experience was critical in my understanding of how to practice autonomy as a kitchen and as a person and how to respect the autonomy and needs of the communities and people I've worked with.

And, most importantly, seeing that community in New Jersey respond and watching neighbors support one another in times of hardship showed me what was really possible in grassroots organizing. Food share projects or relief efforts are, in reality, oftentimes messy, filled with difficult decisions, poor communication, interpersonal conflict, lack of sleep, too few volunteers, very little funding, and unimaginable workloads. But sometimes, despite (or maybe because of) all these challenges, we can create magical and powerful spaces. Moving forward in this work, I remember what this magic feels like when it happens, and I am deeply humbled and inspired by all the meals we've served and all the faces I've worked with.

What do you see as the future of activist kitchens?
I firmly believe that the future of resistance and food justice is, without a doubt, grassroots. Healthy food access and education have always been so inequitable, so out of reach for some communities, and that access is so intersectional with race and class lines. It just makes sense to me that if we're going to envision a more equitable world, where food is abundant, then that vision has to include and elevate the voices that are most often lost in those dialogues now. Who is it in our current world that has the least access to wholesome, healthy, affordable food? When I think about food justice, I think about migrants walking the trails of the Sonoran Desert borderlands, homeless folks, communities of color who live in food deserts, Indigenous tribes who have to drive hours to pick up frozen, canned, and dehydrated food from distribution centers because they can't afford other options. I think about how little food education exists and how little time many working-class folks have to make healthy food at home because they spend so many hours at work, often making food for others at service industry jobs.

But, when I think about food justice, I also think about the magical urban gardens I've seen spring up in Detroit, where remediating toxic soil and growing food wasn't even necessarily a choice—the city was just such a huge food desert that people had to learn how to take care of themselves. I also remember driving through dry arroyos and hiking miles under the unforgiving Sonoran summer sun to leave gallons of water, cans of beans, and food packs on migrant trails, and in each step I dreamed of a world where no human being is illegal and no matter someone's legal status, they are never left hungry. I think of making mutton stew and fry bread with my friend Kerry Begay on the Dineh reservation on Black Mesa, and I remember riding with him in his beat-up truck to make water runs, when we had to siphon the water from the community tanks and haul it back to his house, where we would scoop it up by the precious ladleful for washing dishes or drinking.

I also remember sitting at the kitchen table as a child, legs dangling, happily helping to wrap hundreds of dumplings with my mom, my aunt, and my grandmother as they spoke in Toishanese, a rural dialect of Cantonese that I've since mostly lost. I was in elementary school, and I didn't yet understand how far my family had come or how hard they'd worked to provide me with the opportunities that I had growing up. I remember, too, that my grandmother (who had survived the Cultural Revolution in China) would chide me if I didn't finish every last grain in my bowl of rice, because in her youth, the number of children a family could have was determined by how many people they could feed and how much each child could work in the fields.

Food justice, like any form of activist work, means that we have to take care of the most vulnerable and forgotten communities first. Dismantling systems of oppression means that the only way of doing this work that makes sense is to work in solidarity instead of charity, within structures where everyone has the opportunity to learn from and support each other in an inclusive community. If the realization of our dreams toward a better world doesn't look like the world we want to see, then it's time to stop and reflect on what exactly we're doing.

And, in this work, I really believe that it's so necessary to pause and rest sometimes, and to remember to celebrate where we are in the present moment, too. I don't want to fight for a future where we don't sit down and break bread together, where we don't remember to pass our stories (and recipes) on to the next generation, where we forget the miracles that we've struggled for and won. If food justice is a struggle, food itself is also deeply restorative, and I want to always remember to be grateful for the people that I work with and to remember the dreams that we are always creating. To me, that's what grassroots work is: stopping to listen to complex and powerful stories, recognizing my place and privileges in those intersections, and moving with intention to understand and disrupt systems of oppression so that I can help create something better in its place. Grassroots work is one person, one story, one meal at a time.

What's your favorite meal?

It's so hard to choose a single favorite! I'm definitely really fond of baking, whether it's lasagna, pot pie, sourdough, or cheesecake. There's a lemon ginger cake, modified from a traditional recipe for a blitztorte (German for "fast cake") in *The Joy of Cooking*, that I would bake by the triple sheet pan in New Jersey. I also really love from-scratch all-butter pastry, and I once made a chicken pot pie at the house we were staying in at the time, and the federal marshals raided us while it was baking, so I had to convince them to stop detaining me for a moment so I could take it out of the oven!

I also have warm memories of baking bread with Anne and Victor on the bus at night. We would work by candlelight, and Anne would open a bottle of wine to drink while we were kneading the bread, and Victor would put on Morrissey, of course, and we'd work in comfortable silence. In those times, the bus became a haven for us. These are the moments that are so deeply restorative for me, steeped in care and rooted in a sense of home, even though I was living on the road at the time and to this day don't quite understand what home means. But in those times, I felt at home and at ease, full of a simple joy that I worked into whatever I made with my hands.

Then, my favorite meal to eat is zhong! Zhong is a traditional Chinese food that my grandmother, aunt, and mom would make for us when I was growing up. It's a packet of sticky rice filled with cured meats, dried seafood, sweet Chinese sausage, peanuts, and a preserved egg yolk; the whole bundle is wrapped tightly in banana leaves, tied up with string, and cooked in a pressure cooker for four to six hours. The result is this savory, umami sticky rice snack. Everyone makes it a little differently, but my favorite will always be my aunt and grandmother's recipe.

This interview was originally published as part of the Nourishing Resistance series at Bone + All.

Cooking Revolutions in the Popular Pot

Virginia Tognola

On the sidewalk of one of the typical conventillos, or family hotels (as they call illegal pensions that house families in precarious situations), in Constitución, a poor neighborhood in Buenos Aires, people bring what they have to a giant pot heated over a makeshift fire in the street. Suleika brings potatoes and salsa, Mariela vegetables, Juan Pablo a chicken, and Daniela Trujillo several pounds of legumes contributed by the Frente de Migrantes y Refugiadxs of the Movimiento Popular Nuestramérica, where she militates. They cook stew, a meal characterized by being made, literally, of what you have at home: vegetables, noodles, rice, lentils, meat, broth, sauce—whatever there is with a little water to bind well.

A sign next to the fire reads, "Olla Migrante." In an interview I conduct with Daniela to find out what their work is about, she explains, "This stew is a tool to begin to build a closer bond between the migrant residents of Constitución. It was originally made in different sidewalk hotels once a month and emerged from the dining room of Galpón 14 de Octubre, a communal political space that is part of the Movimiento Popular Nuestramérica, where neighbors and activists on a day-to-day basis got to know each other while chatting in line while they waited to be served. There, it was clear that there was not only a need for a plate of food for migrants, but also to attend to poor housing conditions and the fact that they could not get a job because they did not have identification documents, that they were uninformed about the citizen regularization of migrants, among other problems."

These neighboring hotel dwellers cook in the street to visibilize the main grievance of the migrant sector, aggravated by the COVID-19 pandemic: the inhumane conditions in which owners of illegal hotels house people who come to Argentina without money or contacts to help

Cooking onions in the collective kitchen

them. At the hotels, basic hygiene and safety conditions are not met, nor are there contracts stipulated by institutional regulations, so tenants are left to the good of the owners, who do not hesitate to evict entire families when they fall behind with the rents. These conventillos mostly house poor people who come to Argentina looking for better futures and who have no choice but to accept the cheapest rent they can find.

"Although the main objectives we pursue as migrant and refugee activists are migration regulation, decent housing, and decent work," Daniela tells me, "the pandemic forced us to attend to basic human rights that were being violated in the midst of a health crisis where, in a hotel, you share a room with eight people and isolation is not met, in addition to the risk of staying on the street due to the evictions that occurred even though Decree 320/2020 prohibited them. Cooking the pot on the street is a way of showing the situation in migrant hotels: living in precarious conditions, overcrowded, with appalling sanitary conditions." For people in a situation of social vulnerability, getting together and generating networks of collective containment is vital, because in this way they gather strength, socialize information, and arm themselves with courage to pressure the government so that their human rights resonate. Daniela adds, "Understanding that the way out of problems is collective and that no one is saved alone in the middle of a health, economic, and cultural

Food preparation at the popular kitchen in Constitución

apocalypse, we need to create beautiful and healthy ties with the people around us and to be able to count on them for life."

Cumbia blasts from a loudspeaker pointing down a street cut off to traffic as dishes begin to pass from hand to hand. Some eat standing up, so they don't waste a minute of dancing, others sit in chairs or on the floor, taking the opportunity to chat between bites, and others constantly interrupt, asking that we respect social distance to take care of each other. When they finish lunch, those who were serving food make themselves available to diners for any help they need with immigration procedures, evictions, or anything else. They also make themselves available to talk more about the organization and—why not?—discuss politics. It is after dinner that is the most important moment in the history of social struggles. Strikes, revolutions, marches—everything takes place when digestion begins. The cooks finish thanking those who came to eat, and the rest of those present applaud loudly. Everything that is said is said from the heart and from the need for struggle and popular organization to confront the injustices experienced.

Facundo Cifelli Rega, Nicolás, and Amy—other members of the communal political establishment Galpón 14 de Octubre—come to help clean the popular pot. This galpón worked for many years as a space for assistance, advice, and self-management to attend to the problems of the

Preparing food in the collective kitchen

neighborhood, but since the mandatory social isolation began in March 2020, the tasks changed and they began to deliver at least six hundred plates of food weekly.

Facundo, who is one of the managers and activists of this local of the Movimiento Popular Nuestramérica, also gives us his testimony: "From our organization we had the possibility of starting up a dining room for the pandemic and the food shortage that was going through a large part of society, especially the most vulnerable sectors, even before isolation due to the economic destruction left by four years of the neoliberal government of Mauricio Macri, which greatly destroyed job opportunities and impoverished the people."

The work of feeding so many people is only sustained with the will and absolute dedication of those who come together to plan the menu, chop ingredients, and think up and spread donation campaigns to sustain the work. These people take as a vital responsibility the struggle and daily effort for a world where, first, no one lacks food and, second, no one has to ask for food. This is because hunger is not accidental and has a social structure that enables it to exist, as Facundo mentions: "We realized that, although there was a need and a food crisis, behind that there was an even bigger crisis that gives rise to that, which is the lack of work. If you have not resolved that, it is very difficult for you to have access to

Preparing the pots to go out to cook on the sidewalk

healthy food. Even we ourselves as militants and volunteers from the dining room had that job instability."

Those same people who lend a helping hand to cook are also impacted by the job crisis. Several lost their jobs during the quarantine and began to think, while chopping vegetables, about a joint way out of this problem. In Argentina, it is not news that the formal market does not contain the vast majority of people who need to enter the labor market. The first option that occurred to them was to set up work cooperatives depending on what most of them knew how to do: some could cook, some could sew and mend clothes, and others even knew how to make craft beer, so they set up a textile fair, a gastronomic venture, and a beer-making one to start producing self-managed work. In this labor scheme, logics and forms of production are put into play outside of capitalist exploitation. As Facundo explains, "In cooperative work without a boss, workers can begin to establish other types of relationships among themselves which are more democratic and horizontal, both in grassroots work as well as in leadership and each labor instance. From all this, one can think about work in terms of other human objectives outside of the individual accumulation of capital and unscrupulous profitability."

Cooperativism is an alternative form of work to the formal economy, a labor system that excludes millions of people because they are

Poster announcing the day's menu

racialized, feminized, migrant, et cetera. For all of them, a regular job
is a kind of promise of well-being that will never come, because what
actually happens is that the vast majority of poor people are born in and
die in poverty, and in between they work informally, without recognition
of basic rights. Accepting that the formal market excludes and that the
majority of the population never enter into it is to talk about the elephant
in the room and begin to shape an identity as a worker who is part of
the popular economy, with its various rules and cultural representations.
There, the popular pot is the star.

"As a Colombian migrant internalizing myself in Argentine history
and all the struggles that took place here," says Daniela, "the fight was
always won by cooking in the streets. To be heard only by bureaucratic
means is insufficient, because sometimes the problems are urgent and
there is no answer, so people have no choice but to go out and express
their anger, and that is a way of saying, 'I'm here and you don't fuck
with me.'" In this country, the piqueteros movements—which were
first made up of huge numbers of workers unemployed by the crisis
that exploded in 2001 and then formalized year after year into organizations that push politically with para-institutional methods to reaffirm
or achieve rights—have strengthened their symbols of protest during
the last twenty years: the traffic cut, the chants, the burning of tires,

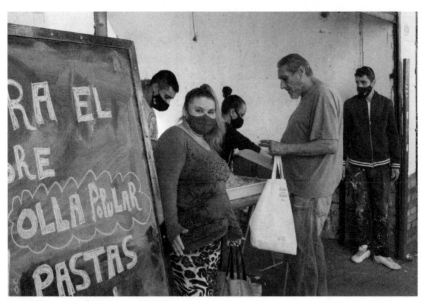

Handing out food to neighbors

the cacerolazos, the popular pots. Each of these symbols has a political and cultural functionality and, adds Facundo, "Here the popular pot is a very important flag of struggle. In the crisis we went through in the 1990s and in 2000, people found there a place of resistance, solidarity, and organization. Beyond the fact that, as a dining room, we are giving social assistance—that of feeding—we are also symbolically organizing and doing something beautiful, because cooking is an act of love. In the pot we are covering a need, organizing ourselves, and providing a little love with what we do."

The goals and dreams anticapitalist experiences pursue are sometimes utopian, but they do not neglect today's needs for that reason. After all, who could plan revolutionary futures on an empty stomach?

In a system of death such as capitalism, social inequalities intensify year after year and relegate many people to a life spent in misery. The organization and collective struggle are a way out of that social determinism. In the cooking of stew, the knowledge of Indigenous people making claims for their stolen lands is mixed with that of those who are on the streets and cannot access their human right to a home of their own, and also with the demands of women who do not want to cook and wash dishes because it takes up their time for politics, and with the migrants who demand that we should not forget that xenophobia is supported by state laws. All the historical struggles against oppressions are part of the recipe. The popular pot is a thousand things and has a thousand meanings for those who fight for better living conditions, and it takes on a crucial importance when it demonstrates that hunger is solved with what we have at hand: popular organization and empowerment.

Photographs by Virginia Tognola.

The Contentious Biryani: Rice, Nation, and Dissent

Paridhi Gupta

Introduction

2020 had just begun and, in the early January winter, I sat huddled under a tent in a remote area of Delhi, the Indian capital, looking in awe at thousands of women who had braved the cold for over a month. They were singing and resisting the Indian government's new Citizenship Act, which they saw as threatening their and their children's citizenship status in the country. As a researcher of women's movements in India, it was impossible to ignore the Shaheen Bagh movement, and I'd been conducting interviews as part of my research for about two weeks.

As the sun started to set, a woman I was interviewing took out a tiny juice box from her purse and gave it to me: "You must be thirsty." I declined politely, saying, "I have my water bottle." Another young woman walked toward me with a small tinfoil box. "Here, have some," she said as she offered me the box with rice. I shook my head, relaying that it was okay. She said, "It's vegetarian, from the langar."[1] I was immediately taken over by embarrassment: while I had refused their offers simply because I felt guilty about taking food away from these women who were sitting out in the open for what was then almost fifty days in Delhi's harsh winter, they had felt the need to assure me that the rice was a vegetarian dish. Their fears and assurances arose from aspersions the ruling party was casting on them, through which the food they served became a site of contention over the legitimacy of the protest.

In 2019, the government of India brought in the Citizenship Amendment Act (CAA), which allows migrants who are Buddhists, Hindus, Jains, Parsis, Sikhs, and Christians from three countries—Pakistan, Bangladesh, and Afghanistan—and who entered India before December 31, 2014, to be eligible for Indian citizenship. Along with the CAA, nationwide implementation of the National Register of Citizenship

(NRC) was also announced, which prescribes every Indian citizen's compulsory registration. The two in combination were seen as dangerous for the country's secular framework, as they allow citizenship based on religion, and as exclusionary, especially with the precedent of NRC in Assam, which left out more than 1.9 million people of over 33 million who applied.[2] While the laws have been seen as threatening for many marginalized groups in India, such as women and trans persons, they are particularly so for religious minorities in the country, such as Muslims. These fears were exacerbated by the violence that anti-CAA protesters, particularly Muslim protesters, faced at the hands of the police, accompanied by the recent rise in violent crimes against the Muslim community in India, such as mob lynching on suspicions of transporting beef. The Hate Crime Watch tracker has revealed that 90 percent of religious hate crimes since 2009 took place after the Bharatiya Janata Party took power in 2014, and at least 87 percent of victims of cow-related attacks have been Muslims.[3] Participants of the movement insisted that the Citizenship Amendment Act would split the country along religious lines and further disenfranchise India's religious minorities. It is seen as an extension of the larger right-wing Hindutva agenda of building a Hindu Rashtra, or nation, out of the democratic and secular India.

As the nation struggled with ideas of citizenship, nationalism, and patriotism with the introduction of the act, the effervescent rice dish biryani made its entry into mainstream media and political debates much like its scent travels: slowly penetrating your nostrils and then your entire being.

The Politics of Biryani

As the Shaheen Bagh sit-in site—which was led mainly by women and began on December 15, 2019—grew in participation and its reach to people, the discomfort of the government, led by the Bhartiya Janta Party (BJP), was visible in its efforts to delegitimize the movement. The party used biryani as one of its political targets to demonize the resistance. Dilip Ghosh, the president of BJP's unit in West Bengal, said that the Shaheen Bagh protesters were poor and uneducated people who were paid and fed biryani bought by foreign funds.[4] Another member of Parliament from the BJP's Delhi wing, Parvesh Verma, accused the state opposition party, the Aam Aadmi Party (AAP), of funding the biryani in Shaheen Bagh for votes.[5] Similar statements blaming opposition leaders were made by

23

BJP's Ajay Mohan Bisht (Yogi Adityanath), the sitting chief minister of the North Indian state Uttar Pradesh. According to the minister, AAP was funding the biryani distributed in Shaheen Bagh, thus fueling "anarchy and anti-India agenda."[6]

While the underlying reason behind the imputations against the opposition party was the upcoming state legislative elections in Delhi in February 2020, the weaponization of biryani worked on multiple other axes as well. Biryani, with its name that "sounds" Muslim, sat uncomfortably on the tongues of the ruling party; they could not digest the thought that many in their Hindu Rashtra were enjoying the "Islamic" dish and, moreover, that it was sustaining a movement against them. As I discussed the antinational biryani with friends, many said that the government was just jealous of being excluded from such delicious consumptions, while others passionately disagreed that biryani could be vegetarian. The question of what biryani is and its differentiation from pulav, another rice dish, is a sensitive debate amongst Indian gastronomes. In her book *Fasts and Feasts: The History of Food in India*, Colleen Taylor Sen notes that the entire range of scholarship on the difference between the two is so contradictory that it is impossible to tell them apart.[7] However, this difficulty was inconsequential for the BJP. Even though according to some historians pulav has origins in Mughal cuisine, it simply sounds less "Muslim" in the North Indian imagination and is popularly understood as a vegetarian dish also consumed in Hindu households. For the majority of upper-caste Hindus, biryani's apparent nonvegetarianism and Persian nomenclature make it an immoral dish that only Muslims eat.

Anxiety over nonvegetarianism is not new in India and is made especially apparent through anticaste debates. Hugo Gorringe and D. Karthikeyan instantiate this with their writing about an Indian national newspaper that posted a notice in its office prohibiting nonvegetarian food from being brought into the canteen. The scholars read the notice as an imposition of Brahminical (upper-caste) taste sensibilities while delegitimizing others. As they note, "The palettes [sic] of the marginalized, thus, are seen distasteful both because of what they eat and because of how they express themselves."[8] The notice at the offices was an instance of the everyday and hidden mechanisms by which caste hierarchies operate with far-reaching impact on who the ideal citizen is who can claim rights. The disqualification of biryani was a similar attack on the ways of being of the marginalized. Identity and food were once again intertwined, where one stood for the other. It did not help that the community kitchen at the protest site was led by people from the Sikh community, or that some protesters insisted on biryani's herbivorous character. The fact that the movement was in a primarily Muslim area and led by Muslim women was enough for the biryani, and by extension the Muslims, to be seen as antinational. One wonders what counts as a "national" food, and who the nation's citizens are.

The Year of Biryani

Shaheen Bagh was not the first political debut of biryani, and neither was it the last.[9] While the end of 2019 marked the beginning of what would become the longest women-led sit-in, of 101 days, in the country, the end of 2020 saw the rise of a farmers' protest against the three farm laws brought in by the BJP-led government.[10] The protesters felt that the laws would increase farmer vulnerability and corporate control over their produce. After months of sit-ins in their respective states, the farmers marched to Delhi and blocked several of its borders. Following the Shaheen Bagh script, the seditious biryani was once again in the picture: the farmers were accused of having biryani funded by antinational separatists at the protest sites. As the photographs of farmers eating biryani went viral on social media,[11] the movement was termed "Shaheen Bagh 2.0." One BJP leader from the western state of Rajasthan even accused the farmers of spreading bird flu by eating chicken biryani.[12] However, unlike the Shaheen Bagh movement, the protester base wasn't primarily Muslim, and the allegations did not have the desired effect of demonizing the farmers' movement.

The relationship between the protesters and biryani also has to do with how the protester is imagined. Among the many anti-biryani arguments, one deemed that biryani, as a lavish meal, was out of the reach of the disenfranchised. The tactic is not new for the right wing: it was also visible during the Occupy Wall Street movement in the United States, where the distribution and cooking of organic food at the community kitchen of Zuccotti Park, New York City, was seen by the right wing as indicative of the affluent social class of the protesters.[13] The protester in the majoritarian imagination is poor and unable to afford food and shelter and is consequently the perfect victim; anything more than the bare minimum of food and shelter turns the protester into an illegitimate person without any cause to protest. It is insignificant that biryani is available at several roadside shops and sells for a hundred rupees or so in various areas of the country, including the Shaheen Bagh food market. The fact that at both protest sites it was made in a community kitchen and arranged by volunteers and supporters of the cause was also of no consideration. The national news channels and the ruling party projected it as a luxury to make the citizens believe that since the protesters were finding ways to sustain themselves at the site quite comfortably, they could support themselves outside of it as well, and hence the protests could only have national disharmony as their purpose.

On the other hand, the community kitchens and the distribution of biryani exposed food as a way through which solidarities could be built. While members of the Sikh community organized the langar at Shaheen Bagh, local mosques sent food to farmers' protests later. Biryani was able to puncture through distinct social classes and religions and initiate conversations between people. Its ability to create a sense of belonging and dialogue was antithetical to the ways of the ruling party, which both groups of protesters claimed had refused to have a discussion with them and address their issues. This lacuna and the concern over not being heard was addressed over food such as biryani, food distribution, and the community kitchen. It's ironic how biryani, the most ordered dish of the year 2019,[14] had become a cuss word by that year's end in the political realm. The protesters have responded to this by owning this cuss word as a symbol of their politics, where consuming and distributing biryani becomes an act of resistance against authoritarian policies. It is an act of coming together in the face of being thrown asunder by new laws that challenge your livelihood and citizenship, of hope against despair. Therefore, without getting into the gastronomical war over carnivore versus herbivore biryani, and turning Marie Antoinette's famous alleged statement on its head, I'd like to say, "Let them eat biryani."

Notes

1   *Langar* is the term for community kitchen practice by the Sikh community in South Asia and elsewhere.

2   India Today Web Desk, "Assam NRC Final Status of Accepted, Excluded People Published Online," *India Today*, September 14, 2019, https://www.indiatoday.in/india/story/assam-nrc-final-status-of-accepted-excluded-citizens-published-online-1599054-2019-09-14.

3   Cow-related attacks include lynching of people by vigilantes on the suspicion of transportation or consumption of beef or of smuggling cows. Harsh Mander, "New

Hate Crime Tracker in India Finds Victims Are Predominantly Muslims, Perpetrators Hindus," *Scroll*, November 13, 2018, https://scroll.in/article/901206/new-hate-crime-tracker-in-india-finds-victims-are-predominantly-muslims-perpetrators-hindus.

4 Press Trust of India, "Shaheen Bagh Protesters Get Biryani through 'Foreign Funds': BJP's Dilip Ghosh," *NDTV*, updated February 15, 2020, https://www.ndtv.com/india-news/shaheen-bagh-protesters-get-biryani-through-foreign-funds-bengal-bjps-dilip-ghosh-2180797.

5 Outlook Web Bureau, "'Shaheen Bagh Indebted to AAP for Biryani': BJP Parvesh Verma Does It Again," *Outlook*, February 8, 2020, https://www.outlookindia.com/website/story/india-news-shaheen-bagh-indebted-to-aap-for-biryani-bjps-parvesh-verma-does-it-again/346978.

6 Aman Sharma, "Arvind Kejriwal Govt Feeding Biryani to Shaheen Bagh Protestors: Yodi Adityanath," *Economic Times*, 2020, https://economictimes.indiatimes.com/news/politics-and-nation/arvind-kejriwal-govt-feeding-biryani-to-shaheen-bagh-protesters-yogi-adityanath/articleshow/73889665.cms?from=mdr.

7 Colleen Taylor Sen, "The Mughal Dynasty and Its Successors, 1526–1857," in *Feasts and Fasts: A History of Food in India* (London: Reaktion Books, 2015), 194.

8 Hugo Gorringe and D. Karthikeyan, "The Hidden Politics of Vegetarianism: Caste and *The Hindu* Canteen," *Economic and Political Weekly* 49, no. 20 (2014): 20, https://www.jstor.org/stable/24479698.

9 While it would be difficult to locate the debut of biryani, there have been many earlier instances of biryani being politically relevant in India. For example, in 1991, the politician Mani Shankar Aiyer, an upper-caste Brahmin, was running his election campaign in Thanjavur district, Tamil Nadu, an anti-Brahmin constituency. According to him, the fact that he could eat biryani proved that his Brahmin-ness was inconsequential, thus making a point for his election in the constituency. M.S.S. Pandian, "Chicken Biryani and the Inconsequential Brahmin," *Economic and Political Weekly* 26, no. 35 (1991): 2043.

10 The laws include the Farmers' Produce Trade and Commerce (Promotion and Facilitation) Act, which according to the government allows farmers to sell their crop to anyone facilitating interstate and intrastate trade outside the physical Agricultural Produce and Livestock Market Committees (APMC). The trade outside these committees, however, is unregulated, and farmers' demands of regulation by the government have been ignored. The farmers also feel that the APMC allowed them accountability from people who were trading there, and the act would take this away. The second act, the Essential Commodities (Amendment) Act, frees up various food items for trade except in extraordinary situations where the central government can regulate and impose stock limits. Until the enactment it was only farmers, farmer producer organizations (FPOs), and farmer cooperatives who could stock items, getting the best price for their produce. The act opens avenues for hoarding by companies and other traders. Lastly, the Farmers (Empowerment & Protection) Agreement of Price Assurance and Farm Services Act creates mechanisms for contract farming between farmers and buyers ahead of sowing. However, the company is not mandated to create a written contract, and neither are there mechanisms for punitive action in case the contract is violated. One of the major contentions for farmers has been the lack of written assurance from the government on the minimum support price (MSP). The MSP ensures farmers with security that in case nobody buys the produce of the farmers in APMCs, the government would buy the crops at MSP. The lack of assurance on MSP entails that the farmers are at the mercy of companies and private players. Jyotika Sood, "Explained: Are New Farm

Bills Anti-Farmer? All You Need to Know," *Outlook*, September 21, 2020, https://www.outlookindia.com/website/story/india-news-the-farm-bills-and-quandary/360640.

11   Also alleged by some newspapers as morphed, where the photograph of the actual food was digitally replaced by that of biryani.

12   Aabshaar H. Quazi, "'So-Called Farmers Enjoying Chicken Biryani, Trying to Spread Bird Flu': BJP MLA," *Hindustan Times*, January 10, 2021, https://www.hindustantimes.com/cities/jaipur-news/socalled-farmers-enjoying-chicken-biryani-trying-to-spread-bird-flu-bjp-mla-101610217359930.html.

13   David Sutton, Nefissa Naguib, Leonidas Vournelis, and Maggie Dickinson, "Food and Contemporary Protest Movements," *Food, Culture and Society* 16, no. 3 (2013): 360, https://doi.org/10.2752/175174413X13673466711642.

14   One of India's food delivery apps, based on an analysis of food orders on the app between January 2019 and October 2019, found chicken biryani to have been the most ordered dish in the year 2019. It was therefore surprising how a much-loved dish soon became a cuss word during the movement in December through the comments of politicians. IANS, "Biryani Was the Most Ordered Dish of 2019 on Swiggy: Report," *NDTV*, December 25, 2019, https://food.ndtv.com/news/biryani-was-the-most-ordered-dish-of-2019-on-swiggy-report-2154109.

La Morada: When a Restaurant Is a Sanctuary

Alyshia Gálvez

At the beginning of the pandemic, we witnessed the failure of our food system. Consumers lined up to try to find supplies on bare grocery store shelves. Food bank lines soon stretched miles. We saw vegetables and fruits rotting in the fields, even as many agricultural workers and food processors were obliged to continue working in dangerous conditions due to lack of sick leave or an economic safety net. COVID ripped through meat-packing facilities, which became hot spots for virus transmission.[1] Workers in food service and delivery in restaurants and supermarkets continued to labor, quickly revealing that "essential" really means sacrificial.[2] Even while news reports and supermarkets tried to reassure us that this was a temporary supply-and-demand issue and that the food system was secure, we quickly saw through that fiction. COVID clarifies.[3] COVID did not create the conditions of scarcity and risk but revealed them, unveiling our food system as woefully inadequate at its primary function: producing and distributing safe and sufficient food.

Into the void left by a failed food system, mutual aid projects stepped forward. One of these mutual aid projects was built by the owner-operators of La Morada, a Oaxacan restaurant in the South Bronx: Natalia Mendez, Antonio Saavedra, and their three adult children, Yajaira, Marco, and Carolina. After the family recovered from their own bout of illness in March 2020, they reopened their restaurant with the purpose of delivering food aid to their marginalized, unemployed, and unprotected neighbors. The Bronx has been one of the hardest-hit locations in the country, and possibly the world, during the pandemic, with high rates of infection and death as well as high rates of unemployment, along with low rates of access to existing relief programs.[4] The South Bronx, including Mott Haven, where La Morada is located, is even more vulnerable than the rest of the borough. To meet this need and convert La Morada

from a small-scale restaurant into a soup kitchen required massive infu-
sions of labor and resources, none more crucial than the family's own
determination and generosity. After some weeks of serving as many as
1,000 daily meals, they settled into a routine of producing 650 meals every
day and continue to do so as of this writing, in January 2021.

How did this family come to do this work, and how is it that if we
are to salvage our food system, it will be their example that teaches us
how? That is what I explore here.

Mendez and Saavedra were born and raised in San Miguel
Ahuehuetitlán in the Mixteca region of the state of Oaxaca to rural,
Mixtec-speaking families. After they had their first two children,
economic conditions drove them to migrate to Mexico City and then to
New York City. Their two older children stayed with family members
in Oaxaca (the youngest was born in New York), but when Natalia
observed the quality of the public-school education children in her upper
Manhattan neighborhood were receiving at the school across the street
from her apartment, she had a vision that her family's educational aspirations could be better met through a family migration project. The
forces that drove them from Oaxaca were the same forces that drove
one in ten Mexicans to leave their country at the end of the twentieth
century. Decades of drought, a peso devaluation, and eventually, in 1994,
the North American Free Trade Agreement destabilized the countryside,
making even the long-precarious viability of small-scale farming intol-
erably difficult. The absence of a provision in NAFTA to facilitate labor
mobility in a context of heightened mobility of goods and capital meant
that, like most of their compatriots who migrated, the Mendez-Saavedra
family migrated without access to visas, and without authorization. The
failure of the US Congress to pass immigration reform in the quarter
century since then has meant the precarity of their immigration status
has remained unresolved.[5] In 2008, they opened their restaurant during
a different economic crisis. In the years before that, they cycled through
every possible station in the food supply chain: farmers, pickers, packers,
kitchen prep, cooking, and distribution. Their lived journey is, in many
ways, an illustration of the destabilizing consequences of NAFTA and
the displacement it implied for so many.

In New York, they arrived to a city being restructured from older
economic models of manufacturing and production to the "FIRE" economy: finance, insurance, and real estate, all inherently speculative realms.[6]

Immigrant labor was the fuel on which the service economy chugged along, sustaining all other economic arenas. But the city's explosive growth of wealth and inequality was accelerated by the foreclosure of access to generational wealth accumulation and even to basic stability for Black, Indigenous, and Latinx New Yorkers. The South Bronx is ground zero for this shift: white flight and structural disinvestment led to arson by property owners that razed 80 percent of the housing stock to the ground in the 1970s, priming the soil for a gentrified economic "revitalization" premised on displacement and disenfranchisement.[7]

Opening their restaurant in Mott Haven, the Mendez-Saavedra family lived through territorial displacement and the shifting roles available to them and others like them in the new economic order. They laid claim to a storefront on Willis Avenue and built a space that would serve as a haven for immigrants while receiving accolades from the global food media establishment.[8] The restaurant is emblazoned inside and out with messages about the family's ethical code. The front door, painted black with red lettering, reads, "Refugees welcome." A banner hanging across one wall reads, "No deportaciones/deportations." The walls are filled with art by local community members who attend art-making workshops, as well as by Marco, a painter, and his collaborator Steve Pavey, an anthropologist and photographer who has photographed Marco for years at demonstrations.[9] They have spoken out about police brutality, and even suffered from it.[10] The dominant color is purple; *morada* means "purple," but *morada* is also a term for a shelter. A place for pilgrims to rest on a journey is *una morada*, the same name used for the rustic communal shelters that campesinxs in Oaxaca and other parts of Mexico use for sleeping and protection from the rain when their fields are many hours' walk from their homes. La Morada is a haven constructed as a sanctuary for immigrants, refugees, and all those displaced or on the verge of it—many Black and Latinx Bronxites—whose futures have not been contemplated in the city's and developers' plans for "revitalization."

It is therefore moving but not surprising that La Morada would become a stronghold and a shelter in the storm of COVID, the ensuing economic collapse, and the nefarious inadequacy of the social safety net. The people making good food and healing communities are the same people who have been most buffeted by violence and structural constraints. It is they who can indicate to the rest of us how to move forward and build a food system that actually feeds us, to take a food system oriented around corporate profits and turn it into a system that promotes health, community, and culture. And they may provide answers to important questions: Can food defy the separation of families by borders? Can foodways help us withstand climate change? Can a humane food system feed us in a pandemic and beyond?

One clue in answering these questions can be found in the philosophy of La Morada. When I asked Natalia Mendez how they managed to feed so many people with their limited staffing and resources, she replied it was like breastfeeding an infant: when a person lactates, their milk production calibrates with the infant's needs, producing more during growth spurts, less during more dormant periods, and double for twins. Likewise, she said the capacity of La Morada's soup kitchen managed to expand with the growing need in their community. I was able to witness this on several occasions. Once, when volunteering in the soup kitchen, Natalia stationed me outside the restaurant on the sidewalk and instructed me to give away all of the vegetables. I wanted details and precision: Which vegetables, in what quantities? Bundled into any certain amounts per person? "No," she said, "just give them away." I asked, "What will you use for your cooking?" and she replied, "More will come." And just like that, the vegetables we gave away were replaced by more donations, so many that the restaurant's physical shell could not even hold all of them. Natalia and her team cooked continuously, using vegetables to make soups, stews, moles, and other dishes, and yet their stores were replenished, not depleted. I do not wish to engage in magical thinking: La Morada depends on a network of funders who provide resources, volunteers who process and prep, and partners who distribute raw ingredients and prepared meals. Yet, by resisting scarcity and embracing abundance, they have been able, in very tangible ways, to increase the supplies available to them in their efforts. Scarcity models are at the root of capitalist food systems: supply and availability are gauged in ways to continuously reproduce demand, yes, but also need and lack. Some have too much—surplus stock, excessive purchasing power, overflowing pantries—while others have too little. The need to continuously generate profits means that the basic needs of all can never simply be met; demand always has to exceed supply. Any temporary "excess" is eliminated through waste or brief bouts of charitable giving, contributing to the (occasional) boom and (often) bust cycles of emergency aid in food banks and pantries. An abundance-based approach, in contrast, operates from the principle that there is enough for everyone and that when we share, we are replenished, not only in terms of material supplies, but also psychically and collectively. This model of resilience underlying the premise of mutual aid offers a beacon for a way to live plentifully in spite of, or perhaps instead of, capitalism.

In the Zapotec language, one of many Indigenous languages spoken in Oaxaca, the term *guelaguetza* means "an offering" or "a gift," or "a fulfillment of a promise." When I spent time conducting research in Oaxaca, my neighbors would stop by on a daily basis, bringing a few squash blossoms or a packet of roasted chapulines. I learned to pop by their house with a portion of the soup I had made from the squash blossoms. The daily exchange of small gifts serves to link the community together, providing a fabric of collaboration and resource sharing that can be activated in times of more extreme need.[11] In a more just and humane transnational food system, sufficiency and abundance for all would be a hemispheric value underlying trade and food policy. Instead, much of our trade and food policy is premised on a zero-sum notion that anyone who is not "winning" in the form of trade surpluses and profits is "losing."[12] But the basic concept of reciprocity and giving without expectation of immediate or exactly equivalent compensation is the premise for true abundance: you have a few squash blossoms, I will make soup, and everyone will eat. Diversity of climate, seasonality, culture, and more could mean that we would have a rich and varied potluck of resources available to us, enabling a hemispheric banquet rather than a food system driven by corporate profit seeking at the expense of all else.

Mutual aid is also a mode of reparations. I write this sitting on unceded Lenape territory. Indigenous people have been displaced from their ancestral lands. The presence of La Morada's Mixtec-speaking owners on unceded Lenape territory is not an accident, but a product of centuries of deterritorialization, forced and unforced migration, and settler colonial violence. Anti-Black violence has prevented African-American wealth accumulation and caused territorial displacement in the form of the Great Migration (the reason why many Black Bronxites came to reside where they do while having family ties to the American South), as well as more recent waves of displacement caused by gentrification and "urban renewal." Mutual aid projects like La Morada's not only distribute food aid in the short term but seek to reclaim land for the production of food. They utilize community gardens and rural community farms to produce some of the ingredients they need and advocate for access to more land so that more Bronxites can have access to food production and farming, including the intangible cultural resource of knowing how to grow food. They have their eye on more community gardens, as well as underutilized land on campuses of the City University of New York, with land access as a form of reparation. Growing food in the Bronx is not only a way of reclaiming territory to produce nourishing and culturally relevant food, it is a form of symbolic reclamation against portrayals of the Bronx as an industrial wasteland, toxic and unproductive, ruined and made uninhabitable by waves of scorched-earth exploitation and pollution.

Finally, good food is medicine. La Morada not only feeds people, it engages in a pedagogical project of passing on millennial Indigenous foodways and knowledge that are restorative and healing. In the fall of 2020, La Morada held a workshop on preserving and utilizing medicinal herbs. It prepared food boxes that included soup along with the ingredients of the soup in raw form and a recipe for making more. One member of the family, Carolina, is a food educator with the nonprofit Stone Barns Center, conducting food and cooking education in local schools. La Morada's owners are seeking to expand the physical footprint of the restaurant in order to add a teaching kitchen and garden space.

Food is an expression and vehicle for maintenance of the transmission of culture as well as a salve in and of itself. In a pandemic, with so much physical suffering from the virus and emotional suffering from social isolation and economic and political crises, food can heal. In all of these ways, La Morada's mutual aid project is a lesson to all of us who want a food system that feeds us, that offers the potential for healing and reparation, and that points to a route out of capitalism's twisted and necropolitical dead end.[13]

Notes

1   Leah Douglas, "Mapping Covid-19 Outbreaks in the Food System," Food & Environment Reporting Network, April 22, 2020, https://thefern.org/2020/04/mapping-covid-19-in-meat-and-food-processing-plants/.

2   African American Policy Forum, "Under The Blacklight: Narrating the Nightmare & (Re)Imagining the Possible," May 20, 2020, video, 96 min., https://www.youtube.com/watch?v=E0ppfjbESV4.

3   Natali Valdez, personal communication with the author, 2020.

4   "Covid-19: Data," New York City Health, City of New York, accessed September 7, 2022, https://www1.nyc.gov/site/doh/covid/covid-19-data-totals.page#boro; Catalina Cruz and Michael Blake, "The Bronx and Queens Are Crying Out for Help," *New York Times*, June 9, 2020, https://www.nytimes.com/2020/06/09/opinion/bronx-queens-coronavirus-racism.html?fbclid=IwAR0mQZ1SuozX6-U7kSeC2dLRmsa6cUxP97t Y7vP6ZuSKNjP7Kfc7dtpdu_M.

5   Amelia Nierenberg, "A Mexican Restaurant in the Bronx Prepares for an Asylum Case," *New York Times*, November 6, 2019, https://www.nytimes.com/2019/11/06/dining/la-morada-immigration.html.

6   Jane Kelsey, *The Fire Economy: New Zealand's Reckoning* (Wellington, New Zealand: Bridget Williams Books, 2015); Philippe Bourgois, "Workaday World, Crack Economy," *The Nation*, December 4, 1995, 706–711.

7   Deborah Wallace and Rodrick Wallace, *A Plague on Your Houses: How New York Was Burned Down and National Public Health Crumbled* (London: Verso, 1998); Vivian Vázquez Irizarry, dir., *Decade of Fire*, film, 2019.

8   "La Morada," Michelin Guide, accessed September 7, 2022, https://guide.michelin.com/us/en/new-york-state/new-york/restaurant/la-morada; Nicholas Niarchos, "La Morada: A Crucible of Resistance," *New Yorker*, September 22, 2017, https://www.newyorker.com/magazine/2017/10/02/la-morada-a-crucible-of-resistance.

9   Steve Pavey and Marco Saavedra, *Shadows then Light* (Lexington, KY: One Horizon Institute, 2012).

10   Kayla Kumari Upadhayaya, "Hit Restaurant Alleges NYPD Arrested Undocumented Immigrant Owner without Cause," *NY Eater*, January 15, 2019, https://ny.eater.com/2019/1/15/18182318/la-morada-nypd-immigration-raid-south-bronx.

11   Kristin Norget, *Days of Death, Days of Life: Ritual in the Popular Culture of Oaxaca* (New York: Columbia University Press, 2000).

12   Alyshia Gálvez, *Eating NAFTA: Trade, Food Policies, and the Destruction of Mexico* (Oakland: University of California Press, 2018).

13   Achille Mbembé, "Necropolitics," *Public Culture* 15, no. 1 (Winter 2003): 11–40.

The Way It Could Be: Toward Food Sovereignty and against State Dependence

Luz Cruz

In the 1960s, Operation Bootstrap, a development policy akin to the New Deal, tried to invoke an era of industrialization across the island of Puerto Rico, forcing farmers and individuals from the rural areas into the cities. The effect this had on farming communities in Puerto Rico is one that is still felt today. This law forced one of the largest migrations to the United States, one that "exceeded the vast relocation of European immigrants to the United States in the late nineteenth century."[1] This, along with Puerto Rico's colonial status, furthered and furthers oppressive structures and continues to perpetuate the United States' legacies of extractive labor and forced separation of land-based peoples from their lands and Indigenous practices.

In December of 2017, I arrived on the island of Boriken, also known by its colonial name of Puerto Rico, my ancestral home. Hurricane Maria had just struck the island, and due to the state's failure, over five thousand people died. Food and water were sparse, and I found myself climbing a ladder to reach a cistern on a roof to fill buckets of water to be filtered in order to cook or drink. My primary directive for moving back to the archipelago was to help promote food sovereignty by assisting farmers' return to their lands and helping them rebuild their farms to a point where they could begin to grow food again. The role that I ended up falling into was one of a trauma doula: imagine your entire livelihood ravaged by climate change, a crisis in which the individuals most affected are the ones who are least contributing to the problem. That was the case with Carlos Lago and his wife, Tita, who live and work on a farm called Finca Tintilla. Carlos was on the verge of committing suicide as he watched twenty years of his hard work disappear overnight.[2] The nature of the work was one of solidarity and resilience: volunteers with a varying array of skills, predominantly from the United States, lent a helping hand to farmers across the island. The saying "Many hands make light work" was put into praxis, and what grew from these efforts was the belief that the people would and could provide for each other—not just on a material level, but an emotional and spiritual one—far more than the state ever would. This became evident later with the discovery of warehouses filled with water and provisions meant for the Puerto Rican people that were reported on over a year after the hurricane.[3]

Upon my arrival to the island, and in visits before that, I had been told that 80 to 90 percent of food on the island was imported. Speaking of food in Puerto Rico, Christian G. Ramos Segarra writes, "The island is 82 percent dependent on foreign production." The secretary of Puerto Rico's Department of Agriculture believes that becoming food sovereign is "an impossible task."[4] Today, statistics say that Puerto Rico produces 18 percent of what it needs agriculturally, and about 5 percent of what it produces locally is exported. Like many if not all governmental statistics, these numbers are derived from information gathered about registered farms and lands that are producing food for human consumption. This governmental gaslighting that legally recognizes only certain spaces reinforces the notion of state dependence that is ever present in Puerto Rico. While these statistics ring true depending on where on the island you are, there is another story to be told about food in Boriken.

If you take PR-52 from San Juan to Highway 7722, which then turns into 723, then 143, and finally 155, you will find yourself an hour and a half later in the mountains of Orocovis at Finca Guaraguao. Here you will find an abundance of fruits, coffee and cacao, leafy greens, radishes, cilantro, recao, approximately six hundred cabbage plants, and so much more. Farmer Tato, a six-foot-tall man in his late sixties or early seventies, can be found feeding about one hundred free-range chickens at five a.m. and milking his brother's cows at around six a.m. with Silvio, a twenty-two-year-old nonbinary individual living and learning on and from the land. At least that's where I found him when I visited in early 2021.

Tato is known among many as an agroecology encyclopedia with respect to farming in Puerto Rico: thirty years ago, he helped found an organization called Boricua and is a staunch independista.[5] His home, like many others on the island, is in a dispersed cultural settlement, a kind of rural settlement pattern where "typically, there are a number of separate farmsteads scattered throughout the area,"[6] and yet the success and sustainability of the neighborhood as a whole comes from community involvement. His neighbor, Juan, lends him a tiller that he fashioned himself out of a V-8 motor. Juan teaches Silvio, who is chosen family of Tato, how to ferment rabbit in wine and spices to make a fricasé de conejo, rabbit stew, a recipe that Silvio later shows me how to make. Maria, Tato's daughter, shows up with a baby goat and feeds the rabbits radish leaves and kale stems from scraps we set aside after cooking our meals. When the cattle get sick, all of these people go and inject them with medicine, and they count down the days until the milk can be drunk so that they can continue to produce the cheese and butter that sustain them.

Tato, Silvio, Paula, Maria, and their neighbors all exist outside of the state, and their growing practices denounce anthropocentrism and forge a bond with all the species that exist on the land, with the understanding that their survival is dependent on them and vice versa. At Finca Guaraguao, planting and harvesting take place during different moon cycles, altars are prepared before animals are killed and consumed as sustenance, and herbal baths are taken afterward to move that energy and help the animal transition to the spirit world.

To consider other life forms from an antiauthoritarian lens, we must view them as our equal—food is beyond the thing that keeps us alive. While our survival is dependent on food, we can learn a lot about ourselves and the world around us by creating interdependence with our plantcestors. A dependence that denounces the state, hegemony, and cisgender heteronormative patriarchy. What do our food futures look like then? Where do we begin?

This ability to hold the physical ecosystem with such regard requires a deep listening that exists outside of settler colonial, cisgender heteropatriarchial norms. It plays on an interdependence that is not practiced amongst those who are not trying to unlearn societal norms. They instead are practicing something else; they are practicing a particular kind of empathy. Monica Gagliano writes:

> Empathy which bears upon the empathizer projecting and depositing himself into the other in order to rediscover himself, a form of narcissism that makes the other a sort of imaginative variation of the empathizer instead, knowing by deep listening has the quality of a perfect surprise pertinent to the moment of the encounter,

not conditioned by anything inside one or the other and, thus, not intentionally pre-determined.[7]

The empathizer is unable to, on a fundamental level, see different species and humans that exist outside of societal norms as equal, which perpetuates a cycle of extractive and anthropocentric views of their environment and bias about any subgroup that exists outside of their belief system. Their encounter begins with a predetermined bias. This predetermined bias is based on settler colonial mentality, patriarchal views, cisgender heteronormativity, and religious beliefs. We are all susceptible to perpetuation of these forms of oppression no matter what identities we occupy, though one might say some more than others. This form of empathy is in fact narcissism. What would we learn about ourselves if our detachment or inability to see ourselves in the natural world around us didn't exist? Could we learn to emulate the softness of dried mullein leaves? Would we be less deterred from confrontation knowing that it could be a pathway to healing, much like the stinging nettle plant? What new forms of empathy could we take on if we removed hierarchy from our perceptions of the natural world?

Learning to speak a common language with our plantcestors, one that is centered around symbiosis and deep listening for the sake of understanding and that denounces predetermined biases and upholds agreements of community care, is another way to dismantle these systems of oppressions within ourselves. This deep listening requires us to take leadership from First Peoples and Afro-Indigenous individuals whose relationship to the land spans time immemorial and whose practices we conveniently co-opt. Our world would look much different then, because we would be moving toward collective healing as opposed to the dismembering of cultures that have the potential to heal us. So often, though, we never get to the step of listening and we choose to silence anything that doesn't align with how we are taught the world should be, because, if we did, that would mean shifting the way we see the world and jumping into other dimensions of understanding. What kinds of ecological resistance could we begin to create if we silenced ourselves and listened to the environment around us? What teachings would the plants offer us with regards to resiliency and the need for biodiversity in the world and in ourselves?

Food sovereignty can be enacted in many ways. Mutual aid, I have found, is the most common one. Mutual aid is a term that was coined by anarchist philosopher Peter Kropotkin in his 1902 book *Mutual Aid: A Factor of Evolution*. But that is not where mutual aid begins; it begins with BIPOC people, from the slave fields to the cooperative economics of Fannie Lou Hamer to the Haitian Revolution, and every act of revolt and autonomy ever taken against individuals and systems perpetuating oppression. That is where mutual aid begins, and it is also in that place where we can learn how to be in community with the earth around us.

We know what the problems are; we know that failure of the state to keep those on the margins fed and thriving, and instead throwing them breadcrumbs, reinforces state dependence. If we continue to see the world through cisgender heteronormative eyes and not through the beauty of being genderful, of admiring an avocado flower for its beauty and knowing that its gender expression varies on a daily basis, then not only will we continue to suppress our ecosystem, we will continue to silence queer and trans people. If we continue to regard ourselves above all nonhuman species and use the power that we have as a people to create a world where everything looks the same, then we are not using our power to its fullest potential and are refusing to recognize the multidimensionality of the world we live in and our problems. Our individualistic mentality, our commitment to the state, and our continual need to perpetuate and partake in extractive economies will be our downfall.

Finca Guaraguao is just one example of the ways in which the rural population has learned to exist in Puerto Rico. During the week and a half I spent on Finca Guaraguao, 90 percent of what I ate was from the actual farm itself. When I think about statistics like that, I think about the multidimensionality of them, how on one end they can be used to disempower people and convince them that the task of becoming food sovereign is insurmountable and on the other it is this very statistic that propels some people into farming. It's statistics like these that fail people, that create the illusion that state dependence is the norm and that to live outside of such a paradigm is unheard of, that push rural communities to the margins and delegitimize their existence. In reality, their existence should be the standard deviation: the movement toward food sovereignty is in many ways a pathway toward liberation. What kinds of power could we manifest with regard to disrupting settler colonialism and capitalism if our basic needs were met? This is how we all survive and thrive. The work of Finca Guaraguao is the work of all of us as long as we all suffer at the hands of a myriad of forms of oppression.

Notes

1   Johanna Fernández, *The Young Lords: A Radical History* (Chapel Hill: University of North Carolina Press, 2020), 53.

2   Luz Cruz, "Crónica Finca Tintillas," Americas for Conservation + the Arts, 2018, https://www.afcanatura.org/week-16-cronica-finca-tintillas.

3   Leah Simpson, "Fury in Puerto Rico over Warehouse Filled with Disaster Supplies," *Daily Mail*, January 18, 2020, https://www.dailymail.co.uk/news/article-7903089/ Puerto-Rico-governor-fires-emergency-management-director.html.

4   Christian G. Ramos Segarra, "Food Autonomy Is Impossible in Puerto Rico," *Weekly Journal*, September 9, 2020, https://www.theweeklyjournal.com/business/ food-autonomy-is-impossible-in-puerto-rico/article_2622ff42-f22d-11ea-a158-d71aa4411364.html.

5   Boricua is a group whose mission is to promote food sovereignty and environmental conservation, being a facilitator for the community through education and training in ecological and family agriculture, local and international alliances, and the rescue and perpetuation of traditional, ancestral, and integrally healthy practices.

6   Richard Muir, *The New Reading the Landscape: Fieldwork in Landscape History* (Exeter, UK: University of Exeter Press, 2000).

7   Monica Gagliano, *Thus Spoke the Plant* (Berkeley, CA: North Atlantic Books, 2018), 17.

The Anishinabeg's Call to Protect the Moose

Laurence Desmarais

Food and sovereignty are two intertwined concepts fundamental to the Anishinabe Nation's way of life and identity. Shannon Chief, messenger for traditional elders, explains that one part of their ancestral governance system is founded on the wampum belt (a form of sash woven with white and purple seashell beads) referred to as "One dish with one spoon." In the center of this wampum is a cluster of purple beads representing a bowl that symbolizes the land as the food system from which the Indigenous peoples of Turtle Island have survived to this day.[1] The wampum was created at the turn of the eighteenth century when many different Indigenous Nations gathered in the Eastern Woodlands, St. Lawrence Valley, and Great Lakes area to make a peace agreement, trying to put an end to intertribal warring encouraged by settler colonists. The interpretation of the belt that is known today is that every Indigenous Nation would eat out of the same dish and with the same spoon, sharing the land and its resources equally.

Fish and animals used to be plentiful. Over the last five hundred years of colonization, with the encroaching of extractivism on the forests, rivers, and lakes, traditional food resources are running lower. While some Indigenous peoples have moved to a completely urbanized way of life, other groups still remain closer to a part-time land-based lifestyle and rely on hunting, harvesting, and trapping to feed their families. Land defense is one way Indigenous peoples protect their traditional food sources and make sure ecosystems are preserved for future generations to benefit from as well. In the northern forests of so-called Canada, control over wild moose hunting is now an object of tension between Anishinabe and settlers.

"You want your fucking moose? I'll show you a fucking moose!"

Those are the last words Chuck Ratt heard before a severed moose leg was thrown at him by a sport hunter enraged by the Indigenous blockades stopping him from entering La Vérendrye Wildlife Reserve in the fall of 2020.

Ratt, his wife, Tina Nottaway, and their child, Sigon, are one of the Anishinabe families who mobilized to enforce a moratorium on moose hunting on their unceded traditional territory in the La Vérendrye park three hundred kilometers north of Montreal.

Following the leadership of traditionalist Elders, since August 2019 the Anishinabe Nation has been demanding that the Quebec Ministry of Forests, Wildlife and Parks (MFWP) stop issuing moose-hunting permits in La Vérendrye for at least five years. They also called for a survey of moose populations and a codeveloped stewardship program. In 2019, Anishinabe land defenders set up checkpoints at the entrances to the forestry roads that branch off the main highway that cuts through La Vérendrye and handed out leaflets explaining the necessity of a moratorium for now, along with an Anishinabe-led management plan to ensure sustainability. A year later, with too little action from the provincial government, they have enforced the moratorium on their own, blocking seven roads at the height of the mobilization. This intensification of the blockade lines was first called by a kokom (grandmother) after the moose came to her in her dreams.

Nottaway's camp was one of the earliest, blocking Larouche Road on September 19, the day before the 2020 hunting season would begin on her family's territory. In a post on Facebook, she explains that the blockade is part of an age-old battle between colonial governments and the Anishinabe, who want to be able to live with dignity and on their own terms: "Where is the justice for the territories that [are] being exploited due to overhunting, logging and mining? This province doesn't have the right to rule over the Algonquin Nation. They don't have the right to dictate our way of life. They don't have the right to remove us from our homeland. They don't own the Anishinabe title! Our ancestors never ceded the lands."

The Ministry of Forests, Wildlife and Parks ignored the Anishinabe Nation's call for a hunting moratorium in 2019, citing a lack of scientific evidence to prove the decline of the moose population. The Quebec Federation of Hunters and Fishermen similarly insist that "the resource is not threatened"[2] by the ninety moose that are hunted by settlers in La Vérendrye in an average year. But the members of the four Anishinabe communities in and around the 12,589-square-kilometer wildlife reserve—Barriere Lake, Kitcisakik, Kitigan-Zibi, and Lac-Simon—know the land better than anyone. An aerial survey conducted by the ministry with some Anishinabe participants in January and February 2020 confirmed what the traditionalists had known all along: over the last twelve years, the moose population has dropped by an alarming 35 percent.[3]

Hunting may be only one of the factors explaining the decline; the forestry,[4] mining, and road building in and around the park may also contribute. "[Some] sectors of the park have log-cutting twenty-four hours per day," remarks Casey Ratt, chief of Barriere Lake First Nation, in a press release.[5] The moose are also threatened by the human-related increase of coyote predators—including coyote-wolf hybrids—and a climate-change-induced increase in winter ticks.

The moose leg thrown at Chuck Ratt hit him in the shoulder; luckily, he didn't suffer a serious injury. On the front lines, tension has risen between peaceful land defenders and incensed settlers. Quebec's provincial police have only minimally intervened, even though angry hunters have brandished rifles, threatened to run over land defenders, and clipped one land defender with a pickup truck while trying to get past a checkpoint.

Anishinabe people have also had to deal with La Vérendrye park wardens from the Société des établissements de plein air du Québec (SEPAC), the provincial agency that manages parks and wildlife reserves. Land defenders have told me that SEPAC has helped sport hunters get around the blockades by running a shuttle service through difficult quad tracks or suggesting lesser-known alternative routes. SEPAC is also offering refunds on moose-hunting licenses, as well as free zone-correction permits that allow hunters to change their license to areas that are not affected by the blockade. Even with these workarounds, many hunting convoys still showed up at the blockades demanding access throughout the hunting season.

Uniting against a Common Opponent

Sporadic rumors of attacks by mobs of incensed sport hunters set a tense but quiet atmosphere when I visited the camp. One evening, we heard that a group of over fifty hunters, gathered at the neighboring town of Mont-Laurier, were planning to plow through the Lépine/Clova blockade, held mostly by members of Kitigan Zibi First Nation, at eleven p.m. that night. Land defenders from every other blockade drove in with reinforcements. We waited for the hunters to arrive long into the cold, foggy night. People prayed and smudged and hoped that no shots would be fired. The riot squad historically deployed to push back Anishinabe protesters in the park—like during the 2008 logging blockades[6]—was nowhere to be seen. Thankfully, the sport hunters never showed.

For Asha Meness King, an Anishinabekwe from Kitigan Zibi, that evening cemented the solidarity between land defenders from the Anishinabe reserves of Kitigan Zibi and Barriere Lake: "That night it was relieving to see how fast the people from the other camps came over to help us. There [were] people of all ages, [from] youth to Elders, and we came together in strength through ceremony during that scary night," she explains. King is part of a group of youth from Kitigan Zibi and Barriere Lake that raised funds for food, equipment, and gas at the blockade camps. "We came together through experiencing struggle together. Everyone had each other's back," she continues.

Another member of the fundraising group, Colten Jerome, agrees that solidarity was crucial to the success of the monthlong blockades: "I had seen such [a] divide within the Kitigan Zibi community, and the [moose-hunting] moratorium really let them put aside their differences and come together as a unified Nation." Clan feuds have been dividing families within the Anishinabe Nation for decades, but the importance of protecting an animal relative helped heal old wounds. "We all came together to protect our lands and their ecosystems, and I personally believe that this lit a fire under everyone and made them realize how we're stronger together than apart," Jerome added.

For the youth at the blockades, the fight for a moose-hunting moratorium is connected to other Land Back struggles. Ryder Coté-Nottaway, another young Anishinabe land defender at the Lépine/Clova camp, explains, "Growing up, I've always been told that we are all one people. Whether you're located in the US or Canada, we are all North American Indians from Turtle Island fighting a common enemy: the government. When one of us fall, we all fall together. When one of us rise, we all rise together."

For the Anishinabe, the moose are a central part of traditional and contemporary life. Being able to care for and sustain a healthy moose population is an issue of food sovereignty; for some families, moose is a staple of their diet. King explains, "Our people use every part of the animal, from the skin on their backs to their bones. We make drums, moccasins, tools such as knives, et cetera. The moose is sacred. They literally hold our culture within their veins."

Coté-Nottaway adds, "Ever since I was a baby, my family has brought me to the bush. That's where I got my teachings from. The land teaches us who we are as Anishinabeg. It has so many teachings to offer. The land teaches us how to live off of it by hunting, fishing, picking berries, making syrup. The land teaches us about our spiritual teachings, our stories, and our science. The land also teaches us our responsibilities and duties. The land is our home and it's important that we take care of our home and everything that comes with it. We have to protect it and take care of it for the future generations."

Similarly, Jerome says that values are carried along with the way people harvest and hunt: "As kids, we are taught how to respect not only our elders and others, but the land as well and everything that comes with the land. I would go hunting for moose and deer with my family every year or two years, just so that we could have some food in our stomachs. I think a lot of non-Native people have this perception that as Native people, we overkill for our own benefits, but they fail to realize that we were taught to kill for what we need so we can preserve the way of life and ensure that no species will go extinct. With every kill, we show a sign of respect, such as placing down tobacco, and say a prayer of gratitude to the spirits that we were able to find and kill the animal. I would say that it was a big part of my upbringing, because it allowed me to understand, love, and care for the land and want to protect it so that future genera-tions can grow up and carry on the traditions that were instilled in me as a kid. It really shaped me into the person I am today."

King comes from a long line of activists. For her, land defense is an integral part of the culture: "We are taught from a young age to protect the little of what remains ours today. The land has always been very important to me, because our traditional lands are being taken away from us and disrespected." The young land defenders hope that their struggle to protect the moose will be recognized as one that will benefit both Indigenous and non-Indigenous people.

Trophies versus Sacred Life
There is a profound difference between what killing a moose means to Indigenous people and to non-Indigenous people. Coté-Nottaway says

that for settlers, hunting is a sport, not a necessity: "To them, the moose has no purpose or meaning other than being killed for fun."

Sport moose hunting is part of a culture of resource extraction and is continuous with the industrial mining and logging that has also scarred the territory. The meat is collected like wealth is accumulated. Often, significant parts of the animal are wasted or forgotten in basement freezers. The male moose's head, with large antlers, is displayed atop cars and hung on walls like a trophy. On the highway leading to La Vérendrye, a roadside diner has for years advertised a *concours de panache* (an antlers contest), enticing hunters to compete for the biggest kill. In the nearby city of Val-d'Or, up until the 1990s, the moose festival was one of the biggest events of the year, with hunters parading corpses and decapitated heads down the main street. In his classic 1982 documentary *La bête lumineuse (The Shimmering Beast)*, documentary filmmaker Pierre Perreault shows how the hunt can be a pretext for something else: a performance of toxic masculinity.[7] Wives and kids are left in town while white men get together at a cabin near La Vérendrye to bully each other, get awfully drunk, and philosophize about the impossibility of men's emotional vulnerability.

When Indigenous peoples affirm their rights, it's an anxiety-inducing reminder to settlers that the settler-colonial project is not complete.[8] To claim their entitlement to the hunting grounds, settlers gathered 2,500 signatures in a petition, wrote open letters to the government, protested on the highway, and were hosted on television and radio shows. On social media, they hurled racist insults and death threats at land defenders. In multiple statements, the Quebec Federation of Hunters and Fishermen asked for government intervention to dismantle the blockades and argued that the blockades caused citizens "psychological distress."[9] King remembers how settler hunters arriving at the blockades even seemed surprised to learn that Indigenous peoples still exist: "A reoccurring response was a lot of anger due to them believing they are entitled to our land, that it belongs to them."

Anishinabe chiefs and representatives have met with the ministers of Indigenous Affairs and of Forests, Wildlife and Parks, and the negotiations resulted in an agreement to halt sport hunting in La Vérendrye for two years and an extensive study of the moose population in the area.[10] The agreement was signed by all community chiefs in the late spring of 2021.

An earlier version of "The Anishinabeg's Call to Protect the Moose" was published in the January/February 2021 issue of Briarpatch Magazine.

Notes

1   Union Paysanne, *"Paysannerie, migrations et peuples autochtones,"* Facebook, April 17, 2021, video, 115 min., https://www.facebook.com/unionpaysanne/videos/1573367589524526.

2   Emily Vallée, "Inquiétude par rapport a la situation dans la reserve faunique de La Vérendrye et a l'accessibilite a des pourvoiries," Fédération Québécoise des Chasseurs et Pêcheurs (Fédécp), September 8, 2020, https://fedecp.com/nouvelles/2020/inquietude-par-rapport-a-la-situation-dans-la-reserve-faunique-de-la-verendrye-et-a-l-accessibilite-a-des-pourvoiries/.

3   "Inventaire aerien de l'orignal de la reserve faunique La Vérendrye realise à l'hiver 2020: Résumé des resultats," Ministère des Forêts, de la Faune et des Parcs, 2020, https://mffp.gouv.qc.ca/documents/faune/Inventaire_orignal_RFLV_hiver_2020.pdf.

4   "Land-Use and Integrated Management," Sépaq, Réserve Faunique La Vérendrye, Wildlife Reserves, accessed August 11, 2021, https://www.sepaq.com/rf/lvy/amenagement_et_gestion_integree.dot?language_id=1.

5   Anishinabeg Tribal Council, "The Inventory Confirmed the Algonquins' Fears Moose Are in Decline in La Verendrye Wildlife Reserve," press release, August 4, 2020.

6   Dru Oja Jay, "Pain Compliance as Indigenous Relations: Inside the Barriere Lake Algonquins' Blockade of Highway 117," *Dominion*, October 14, 2008, http://www.dominionpaper.ca/articles/2185.

7   Pierre Perault, dir., "La Bête Lumineuse," Office National du Film du Canada, 1982, film, https://www.onf.ca/film/bete_lumineuse/.

8   Eva Mackey, *Unsettled Expectations: Uncertainty, Land and Settler Decolonization* (Halifax, Nova Scotia: Fernwood Publishing, 2016); Mark Rifkin, "Settler Common Sense," *Settler Colonial Studies* 3, no. 3-04 (2013): 322–40, https://doi.org/10.1080/2201473x.2013.810702.

9   Vallée, "Inquiétude par rapport a la situation"; "Un territoire public interdit à des milliers de Québécois(es) et d'entreprises; Le Premier Ministre se doit d'intervenir pour assurer une vraie démocratie," Fédération Québécoise des Chasseurs et Pêcheurs (Fédécp), October 5, 2020, https://fedecp.com/nouvelles/2020/un-territoire-public-interdit-a-des-milliers-de-quebecois-es-et-d-entreprises-le-premier-ministre-se-doit-d-intervenir-pour-assurer-une-vraie-democratie/.

10   La Presse canadienne, "Chasse à l'orignal: Accord de principe entre Québec et les Algonquins," *Radio-Canada*, April 2, 2021, https://ici.radio-canada.ca/espaces-autochtones/1782041/chasse-orignal-entente-reserve-la-verendrye.

On Farming as a Practice of Abundance and Liberation

an interview with mayam

mayam is a traveling farmer who started growing food at the age of six on their grandmother's homestead. Since that time, they've cofounded a QTPOC-centered community garden in Greensboro, North Carolina, and spent two years farming in Pennsylvania, and at the time of this interview in 2018, they'd just arrived and started farming in New Mexico. Ultimately, they plan to return to the Southeast to teach others how to farm.

In this interview, mayam talks about the historic significance and sheer beauty of okra; their commitment to a more equitable and, ideally, anticapitalist world; and how their ancestors, as well as future generations, inspire and impact their work with sun, soil, water, and the delicious food that those elements produce.

Could you introduce yourself and talk about how you came to farming as a practice?

Yeah. So, I'm originally from North Carolina, and I got into farming when I was working on my grandmother's homestead when I was a kid. During the summers, there would be afterschool programs and things like that, but I couldn't really go to them, so my parents were like, "We'll just send you to your grandmother's and you'll work with your grandma." From there, I really learned the practice of agriculture and caring for the plants and caring for the soil, and all the different nuances that come with that. And ever since then I've just fallen in love with farming—I owe it all to my grandmother really.

How old were you when you first started farming?

My earliest memories are so funny. My grandma and grandpa owned a little two-and-a-half-acre homestead, and I feel like I've been going there for a really long time, maybe since the age of six. But one of my first memories was riding my grandpa's lawn mower at the age of ten and running it into a tree and not touching that lawn mower ever again. So, I feel like I've been doing it since the age of ten, and I'm twenty-five now.

That's a long time. A lot of skill building and knowledge.
Oh, absolutely. And the thing is, there's always more to learn—every season, almost every day when you're out there in the fields, it's always something new, something to adjust to. So, I'm thankful for that lesson that farming teaches us as well.

In a previous correspondence, you spoke about the Sunflower Center, a community garden in Greensboro that was run by QTPOC. As part of this project, you grew food for yourselves and your neighbors. Could you tell me about this project?
Yes! Just to give a little bit of background, there's not a lot of grocery stores in Greensboro as far as having fresh and affordable foods, especially in the predominantly Black and brown neighborhoods. Greensboro's historically an industrial town—a lot of trains are run through there—and [in the past] they had a lot of mills that would process cotton and then tobacco a little bit further north, thirty minutes north. It was known for industry and textiles and things like that, but once the colleges moved in, it was more geared toward students. Because of that, you would have a lot of predominantly white schools that would have the co-ops and the grocery stores and all these nice fine eateries, but near the historically Black university, North Carolina A&T, there was Arby's and McDonald's and a bunch of unhealthy fast food, liquor stores, things like that. For a while, I lived on that side of town and was noticing, "Oh, I have to bike a mile and a half just to get good food." Or if I were to take the bus, I'm only allowed two bags per person on the bus, which is not going to get me a full refrigerator or anything like that. So, I got sick and tired of that process, and some friends were also experiencing this as well, and we just decided, "Hey, let's start a community garden. We know someone who has a little half-acre property, and we'll grow our own food for our neighbors and for ourselves because we're tired of the structural limits that Greensboro has put on us as far as getting food." We planned, we strategized for about a month to a month and a half, and we decided that we wanted to grow in a spot called the Sunflower Center in Greensboro, North Carolina.

It was predominantly queer and trans folks. There were about five of us, including myself, who would work the land and plant the seeds. We also were in partnership with a Quaker college that would start the seeds for us in their greenhouse. And from there it just blossomed into a center for people who, if they wanted to get cilantro, they could come by and pick it and we would teach them how to pick it. There was also a community flea market where we would sell our transplants to help us generate our funds. But a lot of it was donation-based, so if you had the money, you could buy the transplants, but if you didn't and you wanted to start a tomato plant in your backyard, by all means take it. And from there we really got involved with the community, and people would stop by and be like, "When are y'all going to plant cucumbers?" or "Are the tomatoes ready yet? When can I come by and work?" It was just really beautiful to have input from the community about what they wanted us to plant and also be like, "Can I take this?" "It's here, it's for you, it's for all of us, by all means you can have it." So, it was just a very, very beautiful and enriching experience.

What are you up to now, on your adventure?
I have been farming in Pennsylvania for two years. It's kind of the agricultural hub of the East Coast, so I've really been learning the practices of farming more intensely and adjusting to what it's like in the Northeast, where it gets colder earlier. And, currently, I was on a road trip with some friends and we had a little bit of car issues in Albuquerque, New Mexico. So, I'm stuck-slash-not-really-stuck, because I am loving it here in Albuquerque. I'm working at a restaurant-slash-farm, just doing some restaurant work, but I'm interested in plugging into the farm, if I decide to stay here, to learn what it's like to grow food in the desert. I've been hearing from the locals that it's a completely different experience with hardly any rain and harsh winds and wind erosion and things like that. So if I do stick around in Albuquerque, I would definitely love to farm a little bit somewhere outside of Albuquerque or just in New Mexico so I can really gain the skill of what it's like to farm in desert and then add that to my skill of farming on the East Coast and kind of combine it, mass it together, and make it a nice little sandwich I can share with others.

What is it like farming in New Mexico, versus the East Coast?
I've been asking a lot of the locals about what it's like to farm here, and they're like, "Water is crucial. It's vital." It only rains maybe one or two

months out of the year, so really being intentional about your water usage is something that they really stress here. On the East Coast, we get rain all the time—I remember last season, the month of August we got thirteen inches of rain, and that was a lot. So, I feel like here, if there's not much rain, then you really, really have to be mindful of the water that you use, and I feel like that would definitely just help me in regards to being intentional about sustainability and those practices, and also being more appreciative of the resources that are around me and the fact that if it's not coming from the sky, what can we use? And to just really, really honor those systems [of desert farming] as well.

How does farming connect to your politics?
There's this quote that I love. I call it an old Negro spiritual quote or a Black food activist quote, but it goes like this: "If I'm eatin', we're eatin'." For me, I feel like that really, really informs my politics when it comes to food activism and farming. So, if I'm eating healthy, then you're eating healthy. If I have something in abundance, then you're going to have it, because I'm not going to hoard it all for myself, I'm not going to compost it if I can—if I have extra of it, by all means take it. Because we all have a right to fresh, clean, and affordable food—as well as water, too, that's just something that we are inherited with, with this planet, and what that means is we shouldn't waste it, we shouldn't poison it, but if we have it, let's share it. That quote, "If I'm eatin', we're eatin'," has severely informed my politics when it comes to farming. And it's kind of helped, even when I'm not farming, if I have extra sweet potatoes or something that I got from the store, and some friends want to eat, then I'll cook a big meal for all of us.

So that sort of inherent sharing, the opposite of hoarding something?
Absolutely, yes, yes. And I love to cook, personally. I love to cook for other people—that's a love language of mine. Of course, I love to grow food, so they both kind of go hand in hand, and that's informed my work with the garden, that's informed my work farming, and that's also just informed my lifestyle in regards to sharing food with other people or whatever I have—if I have something that I can share with people, I'll definitely try to do it.

You previously mentioned that you farm to honor your ancestors as well as those who will come in the future. Why have you chosen

farming as the medium through which to remember and celebrate those who came before and will come after you?

That's a good question. Historically, Black people were taken from Africa and brought to the Americas for forced labor, slavery, and things like that. There's a lot of pain in talking about that and recognizing that. There's stories about enslaved African femmes and women who would braid seeds of okra or rice or sorghum into their daughters' hair or their own hair to preserve the cultural legacy that they had from their own country, from their mother country. We see these plants and these seeds here today—specific wild rices and sorghum and okra. So, I really want to honor those who've come before me by growing these things, and also just honor the practices of farming knowing that here in the United States, there's a lot of pain with Black people when it comes to touching soil. I'm really into [farmer, author, and activist] Leah Penniman, and she said something like, "A lot of Black folks don't like to get dirty, and it's not because we want to be clean—we want to be fresh and clean and look good, but there's also pain in having soil on you and what that brings up and things like that." So, I definitely want to honor those who've come before me who have put a lot of sweat and blood into the land when they didn't want to do that in the first place over here—I'm pretty sure they'd rather not have been enslaved and brought over. I want to do it in a way that honors their legacies and puts a different perspective into farming and agriculture with Black folks.

And then for the future, this is a very, very important skill. I feel like with this skill, you can take it anywhere. You can put something in the soil, you can try to let it grow, and you'll learn a lot of lessons from that. So, I also want to have a space where people can learn—specifically children can learn—how to farm and how to grow food for themselves, for their families, and just really enjoy that whole process of putting something in the ground and harvesting it and clearing out and taking care of the earth.

What dreams and visions do you have for the future?

I envision a world without capitalism, because it's super harmful, it's extractive, it's deadly. I envision a world where we acknowledge one another—we acknowledge our gifts, our talents, our truths, and care for one another on a very, very basic level. Going back to "If I'm eatin', we're eatin'"—just something like that, you know, where our basic needs are met. Not by some outside source or system that requires a payment or, if you don't have that payment, then you're struggling, but just a world where we actually care for one another and we actually acknowledge each other's humanity. I envision a world where we trade our stories, our gifts, and our resources—so, if money's involved, it's not something that's life or death; if there's no money involved, even better, that would be even more ideal. And ultimately, I envision a world without extraction, a world where we're not extracting our energy from one another, we're not extracting energy from this earth, we're not poisoning any of our water. It's just a world where we give and we care, and we just love one another and love this planet.

What's your favorite thing to grow and why?
That's a good one, because there's so many things that I really do enjoy growing, but I think my favorite thing to grow is okra. I remember growing it with my grandmother and being a child, ten years old—a little noodle, basically!—and the okra was like five and a half feet tall, taller than me, and it was just shooting up toward the sky, reaching toward the heavens. And these delicious pods that are a little bit mucusy, but that's that texture that can add a lot to soups or is really good fried. And then it's just culturally significant to my people, Black people, knowing that it came from Africa and that it's here. Just the amount of ancestral power and weight that okra holds. Growing that to share with other people and also to enjoy myself—and it has such beautiful flowers, the whole plant's magnificent. It gets really tall, the flowers are super bright, and the pods are like little fingernails, and you can do a lot with it: you can eat it, you can dry them and shake them like maracas with the seeds inside. So, it's a really cool plant to grow.

Is there anything else you want to share?
Yeah, there's one last thing I would like to add. It's a quote that I've heard recently, and it's stuck with me. It's from the White Earth Land Recovery Project, which is an Indigenous activism organization that's all about land management and care and resources and protecting the earth and, of course, not extracting from it. The author is unknown, but the quote that really stuck to me is, "Don't take from the earth what you can't put back into it." I think that is something I would love to leave with the readers—whatever we do, there is always going to be some sort of a ripple

effect that comes from it. So, if we're extracting, extracting, extracting, there's nothing that's going to be given back to the earth, and ultimately, in the long run, there's nothing that's going to be given back to us. So yeah, don't take from the earth what you can't put back into it. Also, I would say that with people, too: don't take from people what you can't give back to them. Just honor the reciprocal process that we're living in, and this beautiful world and all the resources that it has to give us, and all the beautiful plants that teach us lessons and give us food and provide a lot of beauty in this world.

An earlier version of this interview was originally published as part of the Nourishing Resistance series at Bone + All.

"Remaking the Commons": A History of Eating in Public

Gaye Chan and Nandita Sharma

We launched Eating in Public (EIP) in 2003 in Hawai'i. Our efforts continue the long line of resistance by dispossessed commoners everywhere to reclaim the commons. We implement projects and systems that make trouble with—and make fun of—capitalism and the nation-state. We disrupt the "business as usual" operations on both private and public (state) property and remake them into the commons—that is, we create places and practices based on the principle that everyone has the self-activated right to refuse their exclusion from the means of life. Thus far, we have initiated projects at over one thousand sites through spontaneous and unauthorized sharing of goods and skills, including Free Gardens, Free Stores and Free Fridges, recycling bins, Diggers Dinners, seed sharing, edible weeds cooking demonstrations, and more.

TAKE = act without shame
LEAVE = share without condition
WHATEVAS = trust without apology

All of our projects are designed to be long-term, even permanent, systems of exchange. This includes the temporary activities we produce for galleries and museums. We push against the short attention span of art world programming by formatting our exhibitions and events as how-to demonstrations and distribution centers. Willfully unconcerned with notions of originality, the *sine qua non* of the international art market, we freely disseminate DIY instructions for anyone to replicate or improve upon our work.

Our guiding principle is to initiate reliable anarchistic infrastructure, autonomously maintained by those who use it. This method facilitates forms of social engagement vastly different from those fostered by today's neoliberal policies that further expand capitalist markets and lead to ever more authoritarian state power. EIP systems do not demand that everyone but the rich be "self-reliant." Instead, by making evident that our lives are implicated in the lives of all others, we work to dismantle systems based on exclusion, expropriation, and exploitation.

With the exception of invitational projects, our work always takes place without permission. We treat the sites of our activities as the commons. By insisting that no one has the authority to keep us from the commons, we reject the capitalist system of private property rights, which is based on the idea that property owners have the (state-granted) "right" to exclude others from enjoying that which has been privatized.

We equally reject the nation-state system of citizenship rights, which excludes all those whom nationalists or states refuse to accept as "belonging" in "their" society. Instead, we hold on to the knowledge held by so many before us: that the Earth is our common treasury. Through each of our projects, we work to bring about a planetary commons, a social system in which no one can be excluded. No one can be prevented from entering, leaving, or staying. No one can be denied access to the stuff of life.

Since the great majority of humans have no experience living outside of capitalist and state regimes, EIP works to provide a taste of, and desire for, this outside and to retool us to become commoners.

The motto for this vision is:

Take = act without shame
Leave = share without condition
Whatevas = trust without apology

Many people who become aware of EIP mistakenly believe we engage in "community projects" or efforts in "building community." However, we intentionally eschew symbolic representational strategies, and the notion of "community" is one among them. While "community" is often carted out to unite a select group through abstract ideas of nation, race, ethnicity, sex, gender, et cetera, it simultaneously works to divide us. By design, "communities" based on such ideas define themselves by their membership and, in turn, make those denied entry into their exclusive club into strangers deemed unworthy of empathy—strangers whom we are encouraged to hate and fear.

By contrast, EIP assumes we all start out as strangers to each other. Our work aims to make visible that it is the stranger who provides us with what we need. It is a stranger who leaves us exactly what we want at a Free Store, for example, or the one who removes what burdens us. By putting in place systems based on mutual cooperation instead of cutthroat competition, EIP's projects help us realize a different sense of ourselves, one arising from direct experiences and practices. This helps clear the fog created by abstracted "identities" that help to legitimize the violence required to maintain capitalist markets and state authority.

Indeed, the only identity we take on is that of the Diggers. We did so when Eating in Public launched our first project, Free Garden, in 2003. We planted twenty baby papaya trees on a narrow strip of dirt

with intermittent patches of grass wedged between the two dominant regimes of private and public property—both built from the commons stolen from us.

We put up a sign next to the papaya plants. It said:

These papayas have been planted here for everyone. When they bear fruit, in about a year, you are welcome to pick them as you need. We will return to feed the plants with organic fertilizer once a month. Please feel free to water and weed. Do not use chemical weed killers as this will poison the fruits and those that eat them.

The Diggers

The first Diggers lived in the seventeenth century in the place we now know as "England." The Diggers movement arose in defense of the commons that were being systematically destroyed by violent land reforms, privatization, and the terror characteristic of the formative period of capitalism and European imperialism. The first Diggers took their name from their resistance: literally digging up the hedges and filling the trenches that were used to enclose their commons or planting food on land recently taken from them—in their case, parsnips, carrots, and beans.[1] The liberatory politics of the Diggers was and will always be a politics of eating. We became Diggers when we planted papaya saplings and laid claim to the commons. Our work is a continuation of

all previous struggles for the same. We use the same tactics. We make the same points.

We are not the first people to continue the work of the seventeenth-century Diggers. In the 1970s, Diggers in Vancouver opened a free store two blocks from Nandita's house. Since her family had little money, she and her brother Paul visited every day. To this day, Nandita remembers with fondness the white patent leather boots she once got from this free store, two sizes too big. The Vancouver Diggers took the free store idea from the 1960s San Francisco Diggers, who, for a while, also served free bread at a park every day.

EIP started our first Free Store in the suburb of Kailua shortly after we planted Free Garden. It was a small makeshift hut at the front yard of our rented studio apartment. The dozens of papaya plants we first put out were taken in a few hours. People also immediately started to bring things to restock Free Store. Having once not known any of our neighbors, we suddenly met them in an endless flow. Since Free Store "shoppers" strangely sometimes left money, we set up a Free Money box, à la the San Francisco Diggers, who were famous for their flyers asking people to send them their money for free redistribution. To our great delight, people left money and took money, but never all of it.

Following the work of the Diggers' free store in Vancouver, we understood that unlike Santa and the state, free stores give equally to the

naughty and the nice. They serve the needs of those who leave items just as much as those who take them. There are no benefactors and no one is the recipient of anyone else's largesse. Instead, as the users' collective actions at free stores demonstrated, we were all truly in it together. We were creating a living commons.

To make evident the political character of Free Garden and Free Store, we employed signage, both explicit and ridiculous. Through humor and irreverence, participants were eased into engaging in the revolutionary act of rejecting capitalist markets through their mundane actions.

We have initiated and inspired many Free Gardens and Free Stores since 2003. As each came to be seen as fixtures in people's lives, it became evident that each was sustained by horizontal/multidirectional flow. Even though most users never directly encountered other users, they could plainly recognize that each stranger was a part of a Free Garden or Free Store's social system: apartment dwellers used the Free Garden composter for their kitchen waste, and dumpster-diving enthusiasts brought their finds to Free Stores. There was also Loy, a houseless person, who would drop off extra items, including frozen chicken, given to him at the food bank. It is in fact Loy who prompted the launching of our first Free Fridge. And we haven't yet met a child who wasn't immediately entranced by Free Store. Like Nandita and Paul, they too express amazement at the feeling that comes from being free of capitalist markets, even if only briefly. Their recollection of this experience ensures the potential for more Free Stores.

As users recognize the mutuality between strangers, it becomes increasingly difficult to keep the dominant vision of "community" intact. We see that the commons is a place we enter through our labor, not wealth, identity, or status.

EIP has implemented other systems of exchange, each reliant on the strangers who autonomously activate and maintain them. Alongside the Kailua Free Store, we installed the first of what was to be hundreds of HI-5 bins (an anarchist recycling system). Two driving forces propelled this project. In 2004, the city dropped off a blue recycling bin at our place. "Finally!" we thought as we nerdily put in all our recyclables and waited for the pickup. We waited, and waited, and waited: for two sad years. They never came. Secondly, the state of Hawai'i began offering a stingy five cents for a limited range of beverage containers marked with "HI-5." Unsurprisingly, the participation rate was pathetic: recyclables were thrown in the trash because many people couldn't be bothered. At the same time, those for whom small amounts of money made a big difference were forced to dig through trash cans to find these redeemable items. Annoyed and disgusted, we made a simple wire mesh bin and attached a sign with a tongue-in-cheek anarchist message: "HI-5 / Take, Leave, Whatevas..." We set it up near Free Store and added the redeemables we had accumulated over two years of waiting. Voilà! They were picked up. Soon a reliable system of drop-off and pickup was established. The idea caught on very quickly. By our unscientific estimate, over one thousand bins were placed on O'ahu, along with a few on Maui.

In 2011, the unexpected happened. The coordinator of Honolulu City and County's Department of Environmental Services (ENV) called us. Instead of being defensive or charging us a fine, she liked the simplicity of our concept and design and its potential to get people involved. To make a long (and painfully bureaucratic) story short, the HI-5 project was officially adopted in 2013. ENV works with anyone to make and set up bins and provide instructions as well as all necessary supplies. Most miraculously, ENV kept the language of our "Take, Leave, Whatevas..." motto, as well as our DIY instructions that explicitly say to "trust without apology." To prove that they mean it, they do not provide pickups—a major triumph over the irrational fear of strangers!

The popularity of Free Stores and HI-5 bins was due, in part, to the fact that shopping is a familiar activity and recycling is seen to be "goodly." Building on our growing reputation, we decided to start a project that strays farther afield from our comfort zones: Diggers Dinner, an exercise in radical sharing of both food and knowledge.

Diggers Dinners have taken place in small settings among friends as well as in spaces open to all. The events are basically potlucks but with one "rule" designed to keep the capitalist markets at bay: each participant's contribution must be primarily made from ingredients that they have either grown, hunted, fished, foraged, gleaned, bartered, found, been gifted, or stolen. At the start of each dinner, participants are invited to explain the backstory of the ingredients. At our largest Diggers Dinner, among the last of the participants to speak was a tiny eighty-year-old woman. Stepping up onto a stool to reach the microphone, she began by saying, "I read about this dinner in the newspaper and realized I've been waiting for this my whole life. So I went to the store and stole these bananas and these apples." Anarchists are everywhere!

Two other food-related EIP projects focus on edible weeds: WE(ED)S, a project incorporating "sidewalk-to-table" actions that include pop-up cooking demonstrations and tasting, and Weeds Up Front, which uses front-yard show-and-tell gardens to showcase edible weeds found in the neighborhood. Knowledge about edible weeds is timely. Not only are we in the midst of a capitalist climate catastrophe, but everywhere nationalism is hardening, making the planetary action we need more difficult to organize. We have seen both processes at play in the global COVID-19 pandemic, which in very stark terms showed how our lives are made precarious by capitalist markets and profiteering supply chains. Ongoing shortages of COVID-19 tests, personal protective equipment, and vaccines demonstrated, once again, that capitalism will pit us against each other while selling life's resources to the highest bidder.

Both weed projects, like our others, especially HI-5 bins, were inspired by our annoyance. In Hawai'i, as in a growing number of places across the world, a pernicious discourse about the supposed dangers of "invasive species" or "weeds" has become popular. Although the stated purpose is to protect ecosystems, this discourse is applied willy-nilly to anything not categorized as "native." Many people, organizations, and states subscribe to ideas of territorial purity and engage in the actual and rhetorical expulsion of plants and animals (including humans) identified as "invaders" who "don't belong." Many do so in the name of "saving nature" or "saving the nation."

Such approaches—and ideas—are at odds with life in the commons and, even more basically, at odds with continued life on our planet. Instead of defining some life forms as inherently valuable and others as inherently destructive, our projects on weeds identify matters that are life sustaining and work to activate them. In this time when the choice is between capitalism and our planet, these projects transform "weeds" from a threatening and "unworthy" form of life into food. As with our other projects, we intend for this transformation to spark a way of living with the other beings on our planet that brings forth a commons in which no one is disposable or excluded.

Needless to say, all our projects create conflict. We are, after all, making fun in order to make trouble. Those wishing to maintain existing systems voice their opposition to us. Some try to destroy our projects. This too can be turned around, as was done when the state-recognized private property owner destroyed the papaya saplings we had dug into the land in 2003. While the saplings were killed, the resulting outrage from strangers all around us led to a larger, more plentiful Free Garden that was sustained for over a decade.

With all EIP infrastructures, we wait to see what strangers around us will do. We gauge our success based on whether the projects provide the stuff of life for free and whether they shift consciousness regarding dominant—and dominating—ideas about property, identity, community, and authority.

Photographs by Chris Rohrer.

Note

1   Peter Linebaugh and Marcus Rediker, *The Many-Headed Hydra: Sailors, Slaves, Commoners, and the Hidden History of the Revolutionary Atlantic* (Boston: Beacon Press, 2000).

From "Building the Bases for a Different Life: An Interview with Hong Kong Anarchists Black Window"

Lausan Collective and Black Window

Lausan Collective editor's note: *In the wake of 2011–2012's Occupy Central in Hong Kong, a group of participants decided to establish an info-shop and operate a free-pricing restaurant called So Boring in Tak Cheong Lane, Yau Ma Tei. The space has not only provided the collective a means of sustenance in the years since, but has also sheltered it from the regimented space-time of state and capital. Its members were therefore able to sustain their experiments with nonstatist forms of association and community that were initiated during the yearlong occupation of the plaza beneath the HSBC headquarters.*

The following interview was conducted shortly before the reopening of their infoshop-restaurant, now called Black Window, in Sham Shui Po, and at a time in which the Hong Kong government has wielded the National Security Law to crack down on activists and organizations that were involved in the protests of 2019–2020.

As the interview below with several of their members makes clear, their commitment to lived anarchy entails a rejection of the paradigm of sovereignty, which the left and right uphold in their political struggles to seize the reins of government and monopolize legitimate violence to effect social transformation. If constituting a new hegemony produces new forms of domination, then it is imperative to imagine a life without hegemony. Thus, the collective aims to—in its infoshop and in mass struggles—open up spaces of contingency and free play that profane the established coordinates of politics and germinate subjectivities, relations, and practices that prefigure desertion from the social logics of the sovereign political order.

Community and resource hubs like Black Window are more important than ever to sustain the antihegemonic momentum cultivated in the protests. It is in the collective's wish that Black Window serves as one node among many others that constitute the city's infrastructure of resistance.

Lausan Collective: When and how did your collective come into being? Anarchism is more or less nonexistent in Hong Kong's political landscape. How did your members become familiar with and committed to anarchism?

D: We met each other at Occupy Central under the HSBC headquarters in 2011. Back then, we knew a bunch of people who called themselves anarchists and embraced anarchist values. I knew nothing back then, and I wouldn't say I know too much right now. It's really through the way in which we carried out discussions and made decisions by consensus that I became familiar with the values behind anarchism. Not every one of our members reads about anarchism and its traditions—perhaps most of us don't—we just think it's an appropriate set of principles by which to live and work together.

N: I echo D. Some of us are more interested in these questions than others. Also, sometimes I wonder about this anarchist label. I grew up in anarchist milieus in North America, and the meaning of anarchism in America has shifted a lot, you know? It's associated with antiglobalization movements and the black bloc there, whereas in Greece, for example, it'd assume a very different meaning from anarchism in Spain. A while back, the CNT from Spain came to Hong Kong to hold a conference, and they invited us with the intention of bringing us into their syndicalist umbrella. We were sitting in that conference and we fell asleep every single day listening to what they had to say. So, there's this heritage of anarchism and all the baggage associated with it and all the different, polyvalent contexts to which that term belongs. I would say 90 percent of us aren't very interested in those kinds of things. But if someone was to say, "Tak Cheong Lane... that anarchist group!" I don't think anyone in our group would be like, "No, that's wrong!"

D: We actually had a discussion about whether we are anticapitalist.

N: Yeah, a long time ago. The thing is, with our collective, different people would have different answers if you asked us a question about anarchism. But as far as being anticapitalist, everybody identifies with it.

D: Broadly speaking, there are two other anarchist groups in Hong Kong—Autonomous 8a and older anarchists[1] who grouped together in the 1970s. We work with them from time to time, but we have differences as to how we go about doing things. We do benefit from them, because they've established a network for grassroots struggles, and through them we get to know a lot of different people and communities, such as migrant workers and immigrants from the mainland fighting for the right of abode.

N: Hong Kong has no clear, continuous lineage when it comes to anarchism. When we came into contact with 8a, they wouldn't talk about these things either. For me, that's what I grew up with, and for some of us, they read some books about Kropotkin talking about mutual aid. I think for a lot of kids in Hong Kong these days, anarchism is some sort of exotic spectacle they observe happening in black blocs.

D: Maybe some of us were like that back then. We'd browse social media pages of people in black throwing molotov cocktails. Then came the translated versions of, say, the Invisible Committee's *Coming Insurrection,*[2] and it's through reading these books—even though they don't call themselves anarchists—in the reading groups we organized that we feel like our orientation is similar to that of the Invisible Committee.

N: Part of our development has to do with the friends we've made over the years as well. Just by virtue of us having the space in Yau Ma Tei, and before that in Occupy Central. All these friends we made along the way, from La ZAD, Kamagasaki, and Wuhan, telling us what they're doing where they were and showing us what they made and the books they wrote, influenced us a lot.

Lausan Collective: In the description for your Indiegogo fundraiser,[3] you state that you do not aspire toward national sovereignty or political independence, but toward the power to produce your capacities and potentiality, which is materialized in the "collective skills, knowledges and practices that [you're] able to… build, multiply, and circulate," so as to "[build] the bases for a different life, and the means to defend it." What notion of freedom, and what kind of political horizon, if there is one, underpin your political aspirations? How do your commitments affect the way in which you participate in Hong Kong's political struggles?

N: This question has a few loaded concepts. The first has to do with freedom. Independence and national sovereignty is one variation of freedom. As for what kind of political horizon underpins our political aspirations, do we have aspirations that can be properly qualified as being political? Because the political sphere is this sphere of will and the conquest of power, as well as the struggle for recognition and representation. I was thinking about the phenomenon of 躺平 (lying flat).[4] It's so widely discussed in Chinese social media and in the West. I read so much lefty commentary on the phenomenon, especially in China, where commentators were like, "These 躺平 youth… this totally apolitical, apathetic generation. It doesn't form any kind of political subjectivity, and without political subjectivity, you can't make a revolution." Totally old-school, left-wing recipe for political activity. I'm sitting there thinking that they totally missed the point of what 躺平 is. I think it's interesting because it doesn't form a subjectivity, because a political subject is an agent that has will, and then many agents with their wills form a collective will, and that collective will goes on to conquer power. 躺平 is just something that can't be captured by that paradigm;[5] it's like Agamben's concept of inoperativity[6]—a line of flight from the machine of will.

Obviously, I'm not saying "doing nothing is better than doing something," nor am I saying we're caught between forming a will or surrendering it. I think what the gesture of 躺平 signifies is that something about the political model has exhausted itself. Maybe there's something significant in the gesture's refusal to form a will or act in ways that are customary or codified in order to qualify as being political action, and that there's some possibility in people's activity being opaque and unreadable. Maybe we shouldn't get into the knee-jerk habit of coding the gesture in familiar terms in order to unequivocally condemn it and then offer our prescriptions. That's how I think tankies react too, in that tankie-ism is like an algorithm scanning everything and being like, "This doesn't correspond to what I believe in, so this is imperialist," which is just careless and stupid.[7]

Maybe we should suspend this habit to always say, "Well, what should we do?" and focus sometimes on the aspect of not doing what we customarily do.[8] When Agamben talks about inoperativity, he's suggesting that potentiality is always the potential to do, but also the potential to not do something. If we always focus on being an activist, being on the left, or whatever, then we miss the fact that we could do something otherwise than what we are doing. Instead of always thinking, "What should I do?" or "What could we do differently?" what is that little aporia, or pause, or interstice, that interrupts our customary ways of thinking and behaving? In that suspension or intermission, maybe there's a chance for the political machine to be interrupted. That possibility and that potential represent a line of flight, as Deleuze and Guattari say. So, in a way, our collective is interested in withdrawing and creating something else[9] that can't be captured by the political machine.

Y: As for how we participate in struggles, we would usually go and observe what the situation is like during political actions before considering what else we could do afterward. Fundamentally, we wouldn't want to understand the participants in a flattening manner.

N: If you characterize Hong Kong's struggles as being "political struggles," while they're political struggles on the surface, it leads people to relate to actors and subjects inside that struggle in a certain way. Like, in the dockworkers' strike, a stereotypical left-wing way of relating to the dockworkers would be to treat them as abstractions—the rank-and-file workers, bodies representing a mass to be directed and represented by union representatives.[10] For our collective, we would think that the demands they put forward are absolutely legitimate and that they should be able to accomplish those demands. Then that raises the question of how such ends are to be met. Should they be represented by union heads? For the most part, should they just sit around and be filmed by cameras just as a spectacle to signify that they're fighting for something? As for people in support of the strike, how do we relate to those workers? Do we just simply show up with some slogans and banners and say, "We're some university students in support of you," and then parade your slogans around them to show solidarity? How else can solidarity manifest itself?

These are the questions we ask when we participate in these kinds of struggles.[11] What does solidarity mean? Is it some kind of divorce between us as supporters and them as people presenting a set of demands? That's not how we relate to the struggles we participate in. I think that categorizing something as being a political struggle and then using very reified terms like solidarity reinforces this kind of relation. One thing we can say for certain is that we will be wherever mass struggle appears. For us, the demands that a struggle clamors for is secondary to the relations that form between partisans in the struggle. Our participation in such struggles go beyond merely marching alongside them to secure demands, so while achieving such goals are crucial if they are to have the bare minimum conditions for a halfway dignified life, these demands do not define the horizon of our relationship with them.

D: We've shown up many times to support the demonstrations organized by migrant domestic workers, and so we've gotten close to some of the migrant workers in order to really know the needs that they have. Perhaps they'd like to attend or organize some workshops because they'd like to learn, for instance, English. We'd host some classes, and after teaching them, maybe we'd like to do some more things with them. Things apart from what they'd like to achieve in terms of political demands, such as creating some zines with them so they have a space to tell their personal stories. For us, apart from the demands they'd like to secure, which are important, we'd like them to feel they're valued, that people would like to listen to their stories.

Lausan Collective: With the activities you'll be running in your new space—"coordinating screenings, curating our library, organizing discussions and workshops"—do you intend to radicalize more people?
N: No, I wouldn't think of it that way. Of course, part of it is us having a belief that what we do is novel and meaningful—us being together for the last ten years has allowed us to survive. We want to share experiences and communicate, but it's not as though we have something to communicate either, because Black Window is, in a way, us exposing ourselves to the outside, and having a place in which we can encounter other people. I feel like the space of encounter is the medium for, I don't know, radicalization. I don't really want to use that word, though, because I often don't know what radicalization means. Does it mean we form a *Das Kapital* reading group and read all three volumes? Then what? The number of people who read left-wing literature doesn't account for anything, because, for example, our Japanese friends are always complaining that Japan has a very scholastic, academic culture. They have a long tradition of studying Marxism. Lots of kids read cultural theory to do with the far left, and then they make that into a career, analyzing and critiquing things. That doesn't account for anything at all. Also, radicalization is often a code word for left-wing organizations to recruit more members. It establishes a circuit that moves in one direction—there's the radical who radicalizes the nonradical, and this unilateral transmission isn't something that I identify with.

I feel more comfortable with saying that our space is a space of encounter, and an encounter is something that's new and unknown to both me and the person that I encounter, from which some kind of discovery can be made from our exchange. That's why we established our restaurant and infoshop in the first place. It's to encounter different people, or different fragments of reality, which also consists of us going to the countryside in the New Territories to defend farmland or going inside the docks to meet dockworkers. We want to encounter real life.

We want to encounter reality, and reality is beyond our understanding. So that's what we want—transformation, metamorphosis, encounter. That's what we think we can find in struggles: encountering people who are very different from us and outside of our experience and understanding.

If we're going to talk about anybody who's radicalized, I would say that it's us. Of course, through our space, we want to circulate materials and things we've been exposed to, because those things just aren't accessible or visible in Hong Kong, and we think it's important to put that stuff out there. But it's not to radicalize anybody. It's to offer different kinds of perspectives and solutions to problems that we all face, and how we can use these materials to deal with these concrete problems and use them as a basis to experiment with creating different kinds of solutions.

Y: The things we have and will put out are things our collective thinks are great. The gigs and exhibitions we've organized feature music and artworks we think are great. It's unlikely you'll be "radicalized" after you've gone to the events we organized. We just want to put out things we like more often so that more people can be exposed to them.

D: Yeah, the things we like and put out, aesthetically speaking, aren't exactly the most up-front, with some clear-cut political statement that forces you to be for or against a matter. I suppose we want our space to allow for different modes of expression. One thing that comes to mind is, there's a tree that was originally from Choi Yuen Village. When the village was demolished following the Anti-Express Rail protests,[12] the Choi Yuen villagers gave the tree to Ma Shi Po.[13] Now that Ma Shi Po is facing demolition[14] to pave way for Henderson Land's luxury flats, a friend asked if anyone wanted to adopt a branch of the tree. Many people ended up taking a part of it to grow in their own space. In doing so, the journey of the tree serves as a remembrance for an agricultural way of living in Hong Kong that is increasingly threatened,[15] as well as for invisibilized struggles that are just as important as the struggle against the Chinese regime and all nation-states.

Y: We had an alternative space before. With the reopening of Black Window, we could make connections between ordinary people, experiences, different struggles, and everyday practices—how we plant a tree, how we consume—come together.

Lausan Collective: How did you settle on adopting a pay-as-you-want model for So Boring, and how sustainable was it?

D: Two or three months into running So Boring, after we got into the flow of things, we wondered what more we could do to let people know who we are and what we stand for. A friend suggested that we adopt a free-pricing system. If you're a customer and would like to pay, you may want to ask us some questions to learn more about us. Also, in Yau Ma Tei, there are a lot of elderly, prostitutes, and homeless people—it's an old neighborhood and people aren't very rich. We wanted these people to be able to eat in our place and be exposed to cuisines from different parts of the world.

N: Also, we're poor ourselves. I think that has to be part of it [laughs]. We can't afford to eat expensive food. The free-pricing system is sustainable as long as we don't get much income from it ourselves. If that's how we qualify sustainability, then yes. Thing is, we'd only be open for dinner for a few hours every night. I imagine if we had opened seven days a week with longer hours, it would have been sustainable in the sense of being able to generate an income for people who worked there. We weren't able to open during lunchtime at So Boring because the street is used for different purposes. There's a mechanic next to us, and a lot of trucks unloading stuff… it's just not a good environment for lunch service. We never had to incur any huge financial losses. Sometimes we ran into financial trouble. We sometimes didn't open for a few days because we went to participate in the dockworkers' strike or to protect villages in the Northeast. We'd post something online—"Hey, we're kinda fucked… we have five or six days left and we can't pay the rent"—and people would help us out. So I'd say our previous kitchen was very much a success in a lot of ways.

Black Window, however, won't be using a free-pricing system for the entire menu. We will have one entrée that's freely priced and two entrées that are not. We still have very long discussions in our meetings about how the food should be priced. It's a pain, because all the prices are going up in Hong Kong. It just gets more and more expensive to eat out, even with the cheapest meals you can get. We don't think the prices being paid outside are reasonable, especially considering a lot of the food you get outside isn't even good in the first place. We also don't think we're pricing our food reasonably, even though we think our food is going to be a lot better than what you can get elsewhere. We're all poor too. It's a very tricky situation. It just proves that being poor in Hong Kong sucks.

D: We'll try things out for a month or two and see how we can balance our costs. We'd like to gradually expand our free-pricing system if our operating costs work out. Also, we'd like to gradually use more and more locally grown produce. During the So Boring years, we mostly purchased ingredients from the wet market, and I think the vegetables we got were mainly from the mainland. We'd also buy from our local farmer friends when it was harvest season. It was difficult to use more expensive ingredients because we were doing free pricing. We do have some principles, however. We don't use white sugar, for example, and when we buy soy sauce, we'd go for the ones with fewer harmful chemicals in it.

N: One of us is a full-time farmer now. He became one after So Boring closed, because we all had to find a way to make a living to prepare for the opening of the new space. He'll remain a farmer once the space opens, because he'll contribute to our space with what he grows. But his farm doesn't grow at a very large scale, so the amount of vegetables they'll be able to give us will be limited.[16]

D: There's another farmer in New Choi Yuen Village that we know, and they'll also collaborate with us. Maybe we'll explore making food from scratch as well, such as homemade bread.

Lausan Collective: What is the political significance of food? How does it figure in political struggles?
N: I think that in the West this connection is a lot more patent than it is here, because of longstanding projects across the States like Food Not Bombs and whatnot, whereas in Hong Kong there has always been this cleavage between what is "political" and what isn't—that is, the way we live our lives, the activities that we engage in together or separately and how these relate to our subjectivity or indeed our subjection. For example, when me and D brought food that we had made in our kitchen out to the occupied area of Mong Kok in the Umbrella Movement, some people told us that food is an individual matter for each consumer to decide for themselves, that we shouldn't be concerned with how people feed themselves in the struggle. After all, they told us, there is a 7-Eleven and a McDonald's on every street corner in Hong Kong—such are the advantages of being a denizen of a hypercapitalized metropolis.

This is also why every time a mass mobilization appears in Hong Kong what you immediately see is an abundance of prepackaged foods and corporate bottled water—donated by well-meaning people no doubt, and certainly a bun or an onigiri is deeply welcome when you've been on the street for hours on end—though with the most recent movement, people have been much more aware of how waste is managed than they were previously, and this is also why there were huge debacles in the Umbrella Movement surrounding the "carnivalesque" nature of people barbecuing and organizing public hot-pot gatherings in the encampment sites. People thought there was some essential discordance between the affective climate of a "political" struggle, supposedly austere and indignant, and mundane stuff that had nothing to do with this. This is the extent of what is permitted to us; even when we are in revolt, the only subjectivity we have access to is that of the citizen-consumer.

For us, being poor and/or vegetarian, you don't exactly have a surfeit of choices when it comes to eating out, so the basis of So Boring was us having to learn to cook nutritious food for ourselves principally, so that we would have something satisfying to sustain us through long meetings, gatherings, and actions. Then we discovered, over the course of cooking for large crowds in the restaurant, that these skills were transferable in large-scale struggles such as the defense of farmland in the Northeast New Territories, and so on. It makes a massive difference when everybody involved is able to get together and sit down to have a hot and substantial meal filled with nutrients before having a standoff against bailiffs, security guards, and cops in the sun. The meal is obviously also a pretext for conviviality and conversation, for people who might not know one another too well to relate to one another on a personal and informal level.

In the restaurant, we have always treated food as a form of media, but one with its own material specificity. That's why when I cook dishes from the Middle East or India or Africa it's not simply about exposing others to cooking cultures that are foreign from our own, but also about estranging myself from my own customary culinary habits, learning in a very material and tangible way about how other cultures relate to the preparation of food and the philosophy behind their handling of ingredients. I want to be respectful of that and ask that others are too, which is why I tend not to tone the food down and "translate" the dishes to suit local palates. There's also the fact that the food functions as a media in quite another way—to alert people to what's going on around the world. If there's an upheaval in Lebanon or in Palestine or in Belarus, we might try our hand at learning to prepare something from the region, accompanied with a post about what we think about this or that uprising. The music that is played loudly in the kitchen is also a means by which we effect this sort of link. We like playing street music, urban music from different places. It's a very palpable way for people to connect to cultures and peoples and histories that they are far removed from, but at the same time this connection is also forged through aspirations and desires for transformation that we share in common.

Lausan Collective: How was So Boring run according to your principles?
D: We do have different roles, but they aren't too fixed. For example, there is no dishwashing position; that task is shared by everyone who works in the kitchen that night. The lack of strict division of labor sometimes leads to tensions among ourselves. If someone's not proactive enough, they may be called out for taking too many breaks.

N: Yeah, it's just that different people have different rhythms of work. For example, I don't like being out in the front, because I don't like interacting with people [laughs], so I cook for the most part, but it'd be very distracting for me if I see all the dishes piling up and nobody's taking care of it. So when I finish cooking a round of entrées for people, I'd go to the sink and wash all the dishes. All the while, somebody could be sitting outside taking a break and hanging out, and this could generate some animosity between whoever's working the shifts. We're not going to be passive-aggressive and not talk to them for a while. We don't have workplace politics—you get pissed off, but these are your best friends. At the end of the night, after we wash the dishes and clean up the place and go upstairs to sit in the infoshop, we just argue it out. Like, "What the fuck were you doing? I don't wanna wash all these dishes while you're on your shift, like what's your problem?" But then maybe that person is on their period and is suddenly feeling tired and sick.

Once you understand their situation and express everything to get your frustrations out of you, you try to understand what happened that night and how everybody was feeling that night. It's totally fine. In a way, that's how we manifest what we believe in, but it's easy for us because we're also close to each other, and we care about what each of us is going through, and what holds us together is more important than inefficient dinner service.

Y: Another thing is, we have a roster every week, and there should be at least three people signed up every day. Oftentimes, everyone should fill in the roster by Monday night, and if no one has signed up for Tuesday's spots, somebody would get pissed off and argue with those who don't want to work tomorrow. The other thing is, because we don't receive a big salary for our other jobs, we divide the money we earn from So Boring every month after we pay the rent and utilities. Anyone can speak out if they need more, but it's very hard to discuss what everyone needs.

N: For example, after you pay the rent and cover the costs of electricity and water, let's say we have $14,000 left to be shared among fourteen people. Each person can technically take $1,000, but...

D: Some people work more days than the others. But then, somebody needs more money that month for special reasons. Say, his mom gets injured, and he needs money for the medical treatment. But he doesn't communicate that. He just says, "I need much more for this month."

N: Yeah, maybe that person would be like, "I want two thousand dollars but I worked one day the whole month." The natural impulse of some people in the group would be like, "You worked one day and want twice as much money as everybody else?" But, based on what we believe in, it shouldn't be a problem. If everybody else doesn't have a problem with him taking more, then he should just take it.

D: It'd be easier if we knew why he demanded so much, and that person would also feel the pressure of working so little and demanding so much. If he communicated better, things would be easier and more comfortable for everyone.

N: Then at the opposite side of the scale, we'd have some people who work a lot but have another source of income. They'd be like, "I won't take any money. Somebody wants to take my share of the money? You can take it." I spend so much of my time cooking, so I'd usually take more than most people. So, money creates all these kinds of very stupid situations. Money's value is so tied to... I mean, it's labor time, you know? So, we'll always be bound by that conception to some degree.

Lausan Collective: What was your relationship like with Yau Ma Tei's residents, as well as the restaurant's customers, when your restaurant-infoshop was operating there?

D: I'd say it could be pretty random with different people in the neighborhood. Some people from the elderly home upstairs would come down every day in the afternoon when we're still preparing food, and they'd just sit outside of our kitchen on the chairs we put out and smoke cigarettes. We'd talk to each other and offer them soup, and in exchange they'd give us some cigarettes. The people who live on our lane would come down to eat and talk to us about food and other things as well. There's also a woman who collects paper boxes around the corner, and she'd give us so many fruits. She would collect fruits that are nearly rotten from the fruit wholesale market, so she'll select the good ones and give us, say, a box of baby cherry tomatoes and grapes.

N: In the new space, there's an old man who repairs shoes in a very small space next to us. Some of our friends did a graffiti outside our new space on the wooden boards raised in front of the entrance of our new space, which is still being renovated.[17] The graffiti said, 心靜自然涼 ("a calm heart keeps you cool"). The other day, the old dude came by and was like, "心靜自然涼?! 我人生咁痛苦, 點可以心靜㗎?" ("A calm heart keeps you cool?! My life is so hard, how could my heart be calm?") I was painting the whole day and was really tired, but I just had to ask him, "Your life is that hard?" He's like, "Yeah!" and went on to tell me about his life history. I still had to finish painting the wall. It seems like there's going to be many more of these experiences with him over the next few weeks [everyone laughs].

D: We can't really plan to control how we build relationships with other people because everyone has different vibes, rhythms, and personalities, which determine how we communicate with them, as well as the kind of relationship we have with them.

Y: As much as we are aware of Sham Shui Po's gentrification, and wonder what we could do about it,[18] not that we could counter the phenomenon in any significant way, we're not moving to Sham Shui Po with the mindset of diving straight into community work. We haven't really learned much about what the 文青 (hipster) shops, which have been criticized for furthering gentrification, have done for the neighborhood, or what their relationship with the people there has been like. As we did in Yau Ma Tei, we'll settle into Sham Shui Po casually and see how our relationships with the people there develop organically.

This is an edited excerpt from an interview originally published by the Lausan Collective on July 10, 2021.

Notes

1   Lala Pikka Lau, "'The Blackbird Is Not a Legend': A Hong Kong Anarchist Lyric," Lausan, December 2, 2020, https://lausan.hk/2020/the-blackbird-is-not-a-legend-lenny-kuo/.

2   Invisible Committee, "The Coming Insurrection," Anarchist Library, 2009, accessed September 7, 2022, https://theanarchistlibrary.org/library/comite-invisible-the-coming-insurrection.

3   Black Window and Lausan Collective, "At Midday, a Window Opens into the Night," Lausan, June 24, 2021, https://lausan.hk/2021/at-midday-a-window-opens-into-the-night/.

4   Elsie Chen, "These Chinese Millennials Are 'Chilling,' and Beijing Isn't Happy," *New York Times*, July 3, 2021, https://www.nytimes.com/2021/07/03/world/asia/china-slackers-tangping.html.

5   "From Democracy to Freedom," CrimethInc., accessed September 2, 2021, https://crimethinc.com/2016/04/29/feature-from-democracy-to-freedom.

6   Giorgio Agamben, "What Is a Destituent Power?," *Environment and Planning D: Society and Space* 32, no. 1 (2014): 65–74, https://doi.org/10.1068/d3201tra.

7   Mike Harman and Darya Rustamova, "Always against the Tanks," Anarchist Library, 2019, accessed September 7, 2022, https://theanarchistlibrary.org/library/various-authors-always-against-the-tanks.

8   Franco "Bifo" Berardi, "Exhaustion and Senile Utopia of the Coming European Insurrection," *e-flux*, December 2010, https://www.e-flux.com/journal/21/67655/exhaustion-and-senile-utopia-of-the-coming-european-insurrection/.

9   Marcello Tarì, "The Saved Commune," *Ill Will*, February 11, 2021, https://illwill.com/the-saved-commune.

10   "Search Results for: 'Dockworkers Strike,'" All on the Same Ocean 同一个海上, May 1, 2013, https://hkstrikes.wordpress.com/?s=dockworkers+strike.

11   "Give Up Activism," Libcom.org, March 27, 2005, https://libcom.org/library/give-up-activism.

12   "Land Resumption of Choi Yuen Village for XRL High-Speed Rail, Hong Kong, China," Environmental Justice Atlas, accessed September 2, 2021, https://ejatlas.org/conflict/protest-against-the-demolition-of-choi-yuen-village-for-xrl-high-speed-rail-hong-kong.

13   "守田 Protect Our Farmland: Act 1" (zine), June 2016, available at https://drive.google.com/drive/folders/0ByJKt7kH-vDtLUZpZkNCcVY3OVk?resourcekey=0-QYMGodks2K1FW8r23lN8bw.

14   Hang, "致敬致謝馬寶寶," Hamlets.land 阡陌之間, June 6, 2021, https://hamlets.land/2021/06/06/mapopo/.

15   "Insurrectionary Agricultural Milieux," Graph Commons, accessed September 2, 2021, https://graphcommons.com/graphs/e5db6042-847f-472d-9000-34b003a314eb/selection/993f45aa-6e9e-a6a5-4342-b161c0ae79a5.

16   For photos of the farm, see https://www.instagram.com/p/CQdRXlegaUu/.

17   For a photo of the entrance, see https://www.instagram.com/p/CPnjpYUgXej/.

18   無書, "深水埗只是深水埗，永遠不是new Brooklyn," *Vocus*, November 10, 2021, https://vocus.cc/article/5fa910a3fd89780001274cc7.

The Wine Bottle's Intrinsic Blight

Lisa Strid

Let's imagine wine for a moment. If you're somebody, like me, for whom the world stops when you flick your wrist and lift a glass to your nose as the liquid swirls within it, releasing a heady vapor that conjures distant memories and thoughts, this ought to be a pleasant experience. So, let's start there: perhaps with a specific wine, or something more general. Think about what got that wine in your glass. Perhaps you visited a wine shop, a supermarket, even a tasting room. If you went to a shop, did anyone help you pick out the wine? If you went to a tasting room, imagine the space: the room itself and the land that surrounds it, the people around you, and the folks pouring the wine. Maybe there's a critic or a wine writer in your midst. Does the tasting room have a view of the vineyards, the very land that produced the wine? Is there a crew out amongst the vines? Maybe you're at the winery itself, with a window that peeks into the cellar, and you can watch the winemaker directing the operations at hand.

Take as long as you'd like with your reverie and then answer me this: Did you imagine anyone who was Black in this scenario? Was there anyone foreign there? Where were they from and what were they doing? Did you see a woman anywhere? And how do you feel about what you have imagined? Do any of your visions give you pause now?

I'm writing this essay from the perspective of a white, queer, female-assigned person working in wine production, specifically as a winemaker. I have a lot of advantages, and the position I hold is generally one of prestige within any winery. I have certainly benefited, and continue to benefit, from my whiteness. Fascists in the United States—where I live, have grown up, and have spent the better part of my career—are emboldened by four years of being directly called to arms by the former so-called president of this country, news that is utterly unsurprising (but still freshly horrifying) to someone like myself, who lived through the George W. Bush administration's erosion of personal rights and creation of the state-sponsored oppression squad we call Homeland Security. Wine cannot be separated from this history.

The wine industry has a colonialism problem and all the attendant oppressions that come with it: racism, sexism, ableism—the works. In all the "New World" wine regions, vineyards are planted on stolen lands. Whether it's the United States and its pile of broken treaties and the genocidal conquest of much of the North American continent, Australia and its "White Australia" policies that lasted into the 1980s, or South Africa and the shameful legacy of apartheid, it's a tired tale that plays out again and again. Where goes the state-sponsored murder, there follow the grapevines.

It has long been the case that specialty crops in the US, including wine grapes, rely almost exclusively on cheap manual labor not only for harvesting, but also for year-round maintenance such as pruning and suckering. In the vineyards, labor abuses can become life threatening. During years in which fires (and the blanket of smoke that comes with them) have ravaged many areas where wine grapes grow in this nation, this work is undertaken in dangerous conditions with little care given to worker safety. Workers aren't even guaranteed a mask to guard against unhealthy air quality in the best of times, but during a time when an airborne, viral pandemic has meant a short supply of N95 masks across the board, farmworkers are the most unlikely to receive one.[1] Many of these workers are already vulnerable—undocumented, or here on H-2A visas, which are only granted if no US citizens can be found to do the job. The H-2A visa program is designed for jobs that are temporary or seasonal in nature and for which there demonstrably aren't enough US citizens—or enough willing, qualified, or able—to do the job. One might ask what proof an employer must provide to demonstrate a dearth of qualified citizen applicants. If a qualified US citizen applies for the job, they must be hired over a foreign worker. Additionally, employing foreign workers can in no way adversely affect the working conditions or wages of the US citizens in the same positions. For reference, as of January 2019, there were 129,900 unemployed workers in Virginia, where Trump Winery is located.[2] That month, the winery sought to increase its number of foreign workers under the H-2A program by twenty-three.[3]

As many impediments as the government would have you believe there are between the application and granting of an H-2A visa, the percentage granted every year is about 95 percent. According to employers, this is a costly process; however, the initial application to the Department of Labor is $100, and for each desired head count, there is a fee of $10. This is capped at $1,000. For 2019, this would have cost Trump Winery $330.

As it stands, workers here on H-2A visas account for 10 percent of the agricultural workforce in the US.[4] Over the past four years, the number of people on these visas has risen to over a quarter of a million, and during the same time the Trump administration made moves to decrease wages to H-2A workers. Meanwhile, a report by the Centro de los Derechos del Migrante (CDM) found that 100 percent of workers under the H-2A visa surveyed had experienced at least one serious legal violation of their rights, and 94 percent of workers had experienced three or more. These violations include (among others) wage theft, sexual harassment, and lack of access to basic safety equipment. The workers have little to no legal recourse in addressing these violations, and if they are fired, they can be deported. According to the CDM, "far too often the H-2A program funnels workers into a system of government sanctioned human trafficking."[5] This program persists and expands because it is easily exploitable, while projecting the facade that it is a "win-win" for both those employed within it and the employers who cannot find US citizens willing to endure such abuse without bringing legal action. It is difficult to find the number of H-2A workers that are employed in the wine industry, and certainly working and living conditions vary by employer, but given the widespread and rampant abuse H-2A workers face, one must conclude that it is happening in our industry as well. If there's any correction to be made in the wine world today, it should start with placing true value on the backbreaking skilled labor that goes into vine maintenance and, above all, protecting the workers who are the reason we have quality grapes for wine in the first place. All of us in the wine industry must advocate for those among us who are the most vulnerable, and often that means our vineyard crews.

The public-facing arm of the industry has also been undergoing a reckoning. As with the reckonings in other industries that have come before it in recent years, I fear that it will make a splash momentarily and then revert to a status quo—that backs will be patted for recognizing the inequities, and materially very little will change. Female sommeliers have brought forward their experiences with sexual harassment and abuse of power within the Americas chapter of the Court of Master Sommeliers.[6] Black women—including prominent voices such as former *Wall Street Journal* columnist and senior editor at *The Grape Collective* Dorothy Gaiter[7] and writer/educator/consultant Julia Coney, who founded Black Wine Professionals—have been publicly detailing their personal experiences with discrimination and lack of recognition within the industry since 2018, when Coney's open letter to prominent wine writer Karen MacNeil expressed dismay over zero Black women in wine being profiled at all in MacNeil's work on women leaders in the wine industry.[8] And while everyone seems to know about these abuses, only when they're made public does anyone not directly affected step forth to boldly declare that they are wrong.

Alder Yarrow, one of the most prominent voices in wine, noted on his blog, *Vinography*, "How many times have I shaken my head at the fact that every time I see that older Master Sommelier at wine events, he has a different student with him: always young, always female, always attractive."[9] Men in power have a major contextualization problem—every single one of them, from the one who commits the abuse right down to those who see something but don't say something. Once again, it takes multiple women written up by one of the largest papers in the world to finally convince a man that it's time to express that something is wrong, let alone reflect on the myriad times that he directly witnessed abuses of power. Many express hope that more women will come forward with their stories, once again situating the onus of action on those who have the most to lose, who have already endured enough. It's the Yarrows of the wine world that need to start advocating, not the marginalized, because for us it takes critical mass and the biggest platforms in the nation. For him and those like him, all it takes is a moment of morality and speaking out. But they won't. Because it's only after the fact that they either recognize what's happening or feel emboldened enough to say anything.

Once again, picture yourself sipping a glass of wine. At the table next to you, you hear a group of folks discussing their work on mitigating food insecurity in the community. You shyly sneak a peek at the notes the prominent Latinx journalist is jotting down—sweet, looks like the article will be in Spanish. The server behind the bar picks up the phone to inform the person on the line that unfortunately the tasting room will be closed next Monday and Tuesday, as the whole staff will be out in the vineyard pruning. After they hang up, you ask them to pass your compliments for the wine along to the winemaker. "Thank you!" they say. "We all made it—we all do whatever job needs doing and whichever we're most inclined toward at the time. But we were all particularly proud of that one. Would you like another splash?" As you give the wine another swirl, it occurs to you that you don't think you've ever actually visited a nonprofit, worker-owned winery before, but given what you've experienced here, it's great that so many are sprouting up. You think back on a time when the only wines available seemed to be wines that benefited those who were already rich, those who exploited your community and gave nothing back.

This sort of winery—a worker-owned, POC- and queer-staffed, consensus-based organization—is a dream. Sometimes this feels like a big dream, and sometimes it feels like it's not possible for it to be audacious enough.

If there is one thing I know for certain about wine, it's that it has outlived every empire it has flowed through the veins of, and it will outlive those in place currently. If there is any hope or solace to be found, I find it in this fact.

Notes

1 Vivian Ho, "'An Impossible Choice': Farmworkers Pick a Paycheck over Health despite Smoke-Filled Air," *Guardian*, August 23, 2020, https://www.theguardian.com/us-news/2020/aug/22/california-farmworkers-wildfires-air-quality-coronavirus.

2 "Economy at a Glance: Virginia," US Bureau of Labor Statistics, Databases, Tables & Calculators by Subject, accessed September 7, 2022, https://data.bls.gov/timeseries/LASST510000000000004?amp%253bdata_tool=XGtable&output_view=data&include_graphs=true.

3 Mary Papenfuss, "Trump Winery Applies to Labor Department to Hire 23 Foreign Workers," *Huffington Post*, January 19, 2019, https://www.huffpost.com/entry/trump-winery-more-foreign-workers_n_5c4fab51e4b0d9f9be685691.

4 Daniel Costa and Philip Martin, "Coronavirus and Farmworkers," *Economic Policy Institute*, March 24, 2020, https://www.epi.org/publication/coronavirus-and-farmworkers-h-2a/.

5 Centro de los Derechos del Migrantes, *Ripe for Reform: Abuses of Agricultural Workers in the H-2A Visa Program* (Baltimore: Centro de los Derechos del Migrantes, 2020), https://cdmigrante.org/wp-content/uploads/2020/04/Ripe-for-Reform.pdf.

6 Julia Moskin, "The Wine World's Most Elite Circle Has a Sexual Harassment Problem," *New York Times*, October 29, 2020, https://www.nytimes.com/2020/10/29/dining/drinks/court-of-master-sommeliers-sexual-harassment-wine.html.

7   Dorothy J. Gaiter, "Being Black in the Wine Industry," *SevenFifty Daily*, June 8, 2020, https://daily.sevenfifty.com/being-black-in-the-white-world-of-wine/.

8   Julie Coney, "Your Wine Glass Ceiling Is My Wine Glass Box: An Open Letter to Karen MacNeil and the Wine Industry," *Julia Coney* (blog), January 3, 2018, https://www.juliaconey.com/blog/2018/1/3/your-wine-glass-ceiling-is-my-wine-glass-box-an-open-letter-to-karen-macneil-and-the-wine-industry.

9   Alder Yarrow, "The Wine World Owes Women More than an Apology, It Owes Them a Reckoning," *Vinography*, October 29, 2020, https://www.vinography.com/2020/10/the-wine-world-owes-women-more-than-an-apology-it-owes-them-a-reckoning.

Plastic

Katie Tastrom

Some of my friends need plastic to live
Like to LIVE
To breathe or drink or eat

XXX

When you see pre-chopped and packaged produce
and wonder why it exists
And gripe about lazy people
We hear you
(And those of us that can't hear sense it another way)

XXX

Abled people thought banning straws was a solution,
The oil industry was thrilled to not be the target
"Environmentalists" didn't understand the relationship between disabled
 people and plastic.
We tried to explain it but were ignored

XXX

With climate change,
(With anything)
Disabled people always die first

XXX

As if we don't understand environmentalism
As if the very disabled people asking you to please, listen, haven't devoted
their lives to saving the world in one way or another
As if we don't die first

XXX

And the irony is:

We are the ones who use the least resources,
We are not a burden to the earth, we are the ones saving it.
We are saving it by destroying capitalism,
By existing in bodies that by their nature resist it.

Disabled people can't maintain the status quo if we tried,
Which is exactly why you need to listen to us
Our bodyminds testaments to deviation
Of a norm that only exists in the capitalist imagination

Even with our plastic,
Disabled people generally have smaller carbon footprints than abled
people
Because we are forced into poverty

XXX

With poverty,
(With anything)
Disabled people always die first

XXX

Even radicals, who should have known better
because nothing that makes actual change would be this easy
What I mean is: The revolution isn't a change that a Starbucks can make
What I mean is: Listen to disabled people!!!!!

XXX

Just bring your own they say
But who even knows when paratransit will be here
And cognitive and mental health issues don't work like that
And if you forget, are you supposed to be dehydrated?

XXX

With isolation,
(with anything)
Disabled people always die first

XXX

As I write this, COVID-19 is rampant
When the pandemic first hit,
my friends who use ventilators were terrified they would be taken away.
And it once again proved that

With pandemics,
(With anything)
Disabled people always die first

XXX

I could write an essay here about why banning straws is bad

It defines environmental problems (and solutions) as neoliberal issues
of individual behavior instead of systemic;
It's not actually helpful because almost all of the waste that ends up in
the water isn't from the US, it's from countries with less regulations;
The resources wasted on those campaigns could have been spent on
something that would have actual impact on climate change;
People think that not using straws actually makes a difference and don't
seek out actual opportunities to make changes.

It's not just that straw bans don't work
It actually makes things worse
I could go on, but what I mean is:
I hope saving those five fucking sea turtles was worth losing the trust of
all your disabled friends.

XXXX

And it's just a straw they say, which is the whole point.
The straw is just a straw, but we are people.

Recognizing wholeness is one of ten disability justice principles
Because in the top ten things we need to do is remind people that we
are people.

XXX

We beg you
"Please," we say, "this is pointless and hurting us."
And like white people everywhere,
Nevertheless you persisted
Is this what you meant to do?

XXXX

The message is clear: Save the earth
The message is clear: Who cares about disabled people?
I guess we are not part of the earth you are trying to save
Maybe I am on a different planet, I sometimes wish I was

Because on this planet,
(With anything)
Disabled people always die first

On Fat Activism and the Power
of Being an Outsider

an interview with Virgie Tovar

Virgie Tovar is the author of The Self-Love Revolution: Radical Body Positivity for Girls of Color *and* You Have the Right to Remain Fat. *She hosts the podcast* Rebel Eaters Club, *is a contributor for Forbes.com, and started the hashtag campaign #LoseHateNotWeight. She lives in San Francisco.*

In 2019, Tovar and I spoke about the fatphobic roots of the Presidential Physical Fitness Test, the power that can sometimes come from existing on the margins, and the sheer deliciousness of pie, tiramisu, and matcha-based desserts.

You're an author, activist, and leading expert and lecturer on weight-based discrimination and body image. How did you come to do this work?

I've always been fat and always lived in a culture that hates fat people. That has informed my work, but my work really started in grad school.

I was interested in exploring how body size affected gender development. This was inspired in part because growing up I felt a lot of gender confusion, because I was assigned female at birth and I identified as a girl but people didn't treat me the way that I saw girls being treated on television and in movies, or like the thinner girls who were my classmates. I found that boys treated me not quite like a boy, but not quite like a girl either. They were rougher with me, they were more crass, they were more physically engaged in a more abusive way. For instance, there's an understanding that you're not supposed to hit a girl, but as a fat girl I would get punched and things like that by boys and roughhoused with, in a not very friendly way. I grew up understanding that girls were treated like they were dainty flowers, and I was never treated that way because I was big. It really informed my gender development over my lifetime, and I was curious about exploring whether that was true for other people.

So, I went about interviewing women and seeing how that manifested, and through the preparation for that work, I had to read up on all of the literature related to the study of fatness. At that time, the body of literature was very small. There were probably a tiny handful of blogs on the topic, but I had not heard about them before that point. Instagram hadn't even been invented yet. And then in terms of scholarship, there was very little, like a handful of books, a handful of articles. I had that to sort through and it really took me down a rabbit hole, and as part of the background of the research, I ended up by pure chance stumbling upon a community of fat activists who lived in my neighborhood, in my area. They really changed my life and changed my mind. Before I even finished graduate school, I had a book contract to edit an anthology on the topic of fatness and I was already being asked to speak on this topic at universities, because there were, even globally, a tiny handful of people who had done any background work on this, any academic work. That was how my career really began. I feel like I quickly went from being an activist and having a really big personal transformation to almost immediately beginning to talk about it in a public setting and trying to make a social impact, and those things felt completely seamless to me. So that's sort of how I came to the work.

Much of your work centers on fat activism and pushing back against diet culture. In _You Have the Right to Remain Fat_, you write, "Dieting maps seamlessly onto the pre-existing American narratives of failure and success as individual endeavors." How does the United States' particular brand of capitalism—alongside other forms of oppression like racism, patriarchy, and xenophobia—pave the way for and amplify diet culture and fatphobia?

Neoliberalism is a big part of American ideology. I was reading a _The Guardian_ article by George Monbiot before this interview, and it described it as such: "Neoliberalism sees competition as the defining characteristic of human relations. It redefines citizens as consumers, whose democratic choices are best exercised by buying and selling, a process that rewards merit and punishes inefficiency. It maintains that 'the market' delivers benefits that could never be achieved by planning."[1] The way I'd describe it in one word is bootstrapping: the myth that anyone can have anything as long as they want it badly enough. When it comes to diet culture and fatphobia, being higher weight is considered very negative in our culture.

Fat people are abused for being fat and are also blamed for that abuse. The neoliberal response to abuse is that it's not the culture's job to become more just and less bigoted, it's the deviant individual's job to assimilate into cultural expectations. We see this in the way anti-Blackness and racism generally manifest in the expectation that people of color behave in a way that is nonthreatening and conveys an understanding of our inferiority. We see this in the way that disabled people are expected to become as close to able-bodied as they possibly can be. And for fat people, dieting is the way that we are supposed to express that we understand that being fat is wrong and we will give up considerable amounts of time, joy, and dignity in order to show the culture that we are trying to adhere to its expectations of the right kind of body, the right kind of person.

I'm thinking of the adoption of the Presidential Physical Fitness Tests under Eisenhower in the 1950s, which were maintained until just a few years ago and asked school-age children to complete a series of physical tasks, like pull-ups, to allegedly gauge their fitness. But that wasn't really the whole story. Eisenhower decided to propose the test after meeting two Swiss fitness activists who were offering a fitness test to children in Europe. They tested four thousand US kids and three thousand kids from Switzerland, Austria, and Italy. Of the US kids, 58 percent failed it—as compared to 8 percent of European kids. Eisenhower freaked out, and the version of the test he ultimately spearheaded was much closer to military training exercises, testing kids' ability to throw a softball, for instance, which was meant to mimic practicing throwing a grenade. Kennedy would go on to promote the tests, saying, "The need for increased attention to physical fitness is clearly established. The Government cannot compel us to act, but Freedom demands it." I mean, it's arguable, but I see "Freedom" as a reference to military power.

So, you see the bait and switch here: we're using the word "fitness" but we're actually talking about having a military-ready citizenship base we need to prepare from childhood. This kind of linguistic coding is really common when we're looking at something like fatphobia or diet culture. We're saying, "We just want you to be healthy," but that one word might mean a lot of things.

Toward the end of *You Have the Right to Remain Fat*, you write, "According to the culture, my life mattered less because I wasn't a 'fuckable commodity,' and so I was pushed to the margins—a glorious

and strange borderland, as Gloria Anzaldúa called it.... I wish every-one had access to that wondrous outcast world, and I wish the terms of that access weren't so barbaric." What power do you find in the margins? How has that outcast world inspired and influenced your writing and activism?

My work would not be what it is without that outcast world. The margins are where all the people who either can't conform or don't want to live. At this point I just look at mainstream culture and see a pulsing ball of trauma and really unacceptable, sad, often harmful behavior. I say "trauma" because I don't know what else to call the reality of being locked into a life where you live by the rules of homogeneity and normalcy and hierarchy *all the time*. But a long time ago I used to look at it and see glamor and success. I used to look at it and hate myself for not being able to fit into it.

I think being fat—being an outsider—gave me a *totally* different vantage point than people who fit better. I saw boys and men differently because they didn't feel they needed to hide their true selves or their worst selves from me. So, I intuitively developed a critique of misogyny and heteromasculinity before I even had words for it. I saw Christianity, and I think because I was an other, I saw it as a farce before others did. I also frankly... I can't tell you how grateful I am that I think my fat saved me from just becoming some douchebag's wife. I remember seeing my more socially acceptable classmates get picked off and claimed as quickly as possible by the most dominant young men around us. A lot of them didn't get to do the things I got to do because I wasn't the "right" kind of wife or girlfriend—that is, I didn't have the kind of body that men could show off to other men as a sign of their success.

I think this is often surprising for people to hear, but I attribute a lot of my more sophisticated and cosmopolitan characteristics and tastes to being fat. Like—and I mention this in [*You Have the Right to Remain Fat*]—because none of the boys at school wanted to date me, I looked outside of school and started dating businessmen right away. And though of course it was not okay that grown businessmen were trying to date a seventeen- or eighteen-year-old, I was a distressed, horny teenager who didn't know what else to do. And that did kick off an early start to things like fine dining and nice hotels and huge bathtubs and travel—because they had disposable income. Things that transformed and elevated my expectations of life outside my small, conservative suburb.

Because normative culture wasn't doing much for me, it gave me a freedom to explore and no one cared much. I got to sexually experiment and travel and be a nerd and hang out with other weirdos. And as I grew older, I became exposed to different people who didn't see the world in that horrible, narrow way. And those people became my friends, my community, my dating pool.

My work and my activism, my writing, would not be where it is without access to really intimate relationships with people on the margins and being a full-time citizen of those margins. Specifically, when I was introduced to antiassimilation as an idea, that really changed the game for me in every possible way. It was really through proximity to queer community and queer people that that became not only an idea that felt possible, but more than that it became a methodology for thriving, and that really changed everything. My writing really reflects that.

One of the things people don't know about fat activism is that fat activism emerged completely in step with queer politics. The specific way in which that activism looks today is completely circumscribed by that reality. People don't realize that a lot of the codes and aesthetics that fat liberation and body positivity deploy are very derivative of queer culture. I think of something like the crop top, right? Early fat acceptance, the first "established moment" of that activism, was 1969, when the National Association to Advance Fat Acceptance was established, and their whole thing was like, "We want to be normal. We want to get laws that help us be normal people. We want to be accepted." And quickly thereafter, just like a year later about, a more queer-led antiassimilationist chapter opened, and they ultimately decided to leave NAAFA after causing a little bit of a buzz because they were actually much more radical. They didn't want acceptance. They wanted to thrive on their own terms, and they saw mainstream culture and absorption into mainstream culture as not exactly a win or a sign of success, because they were like, "Well, the culture is still homophobic. The culture is still imprisoning people. The culture is still preoccupied with military power. We're not interested in being absorbed in that." What's interesting is—and again, I think people don't realize this, right?—the fact that one of the first things we saw publicly was fat women wearing bikinis and wearing crop tops: that is antiassimilation. Fat visibility could have looked any number of ways: it could have looked like fat people dressing in a way that felt very comfortable to mainstream culture and that could signal, "Hey, we're looking to become part of you on your terms." This other thing, with all the crop tops and all that, that is signaling—whether people know it or not—"No, we're not accepting our place within your culture, on your terms. These are our terms." And that's a very queer act.

For me, the moment of transformation where I dedicated my life to fat liberation truly, as a scholar and a writer and an activist and a person, was when I saw fat women not just passing as normal, but when I saw them thriving in all caps in a way that was super unapologetic and kind of aggressive. That kind of stuff does not emerge from normcore culture. It emerges from the margins.

You describe yourself as a cyberfeminist, and social media, including Instagram, seems to be a facet of your activist and cultural work. What role does social media play in fat activism movements, and what are some of its potentials and limitations?
Social media really gave fat people the power to author their own story and representation. Before social media, it was typically people with fat-negative and bigoted views who were creating all the representations of fat people. They cast us as idiotic, slovenly, immoral, or evil (think of Ursula from *The Little Mermaid* or Stromboli in *Pinocchio*), as undesirable or asexual (think of the fat best friend whose only job is to support the thin main character), or as hypersexual or chasing love but terrifying (think of Miss Piggy), as lacking in style, et cetera.

Social media gave us—certainly me—a platform where we could disseminate information about fatphobia and gave us a global platform to talk to one another. We no longer had to be the one fat person in our community struggling alone. We could now see that we were all experiencing the same things and it was bullshit.

I would say the limitations are the ways in which, increasingly, social media is being pushed to follow the very same hierarchical capitalist rules of the stifling reality that was happening in a lot of ways before social media. I feel like it's really easy for social media to kind of fall into those trappings again, certainly as the plus-sized industry and this issue are becoming increasingly visible and of interest to markets. The ways in which you take a community that has been consistently denied access, humanity, and visibility and you offer them access to just a little bit of that. I think that for a lot of us it's very alluring. We might be very critical of it and yet... I often think of marginalized people's relationship to the culture as one of the family that hasn't protected them. I'm somebody who has moved away from my own family, my birth family, and yet there's this magnetic power, I can know everything inside and out of what's wrong with my family and how they hurt me, and yet there's always going to be a part of me that wants to be brought into that loving embrace. I think for marginalized people, we experience that duality in a really powerful way. We know that this culture, this patriarchy, whatever, has hurt us and will continue to do so, and yet there's some part of us that's like, "Oh my God, for a minute, can I step out of being a marginalized person and experience the perhaps-toxic embrace of this thing that I still feel a deep connection to?" I think it's important for us to be really aware of that dynamic and really compassionate about that dynamic.

As anything becomes visible to the market, there becomes this increasing pressure to bring that thing into the very problematic things that created the problem in the first place. I just was having lunch with a fat friend who's long been in fat activism, and she was telling me how tired she is that every single post of every person who's tagging #plus-size is essentially an ad at this point. Because all of these companies are sending influencers—no matter how large or small their following—free clothing. She's someone who owns a small plus-size boutique, and she's saying, "Oh my God, I can't compete with enormous companies that are using unethical labor. There's no way I can, price-wise, compete with these people. And their ability to give out all this clothing or offer it at a very cheap price is making it impossible for me, as a fat person who owns a small business, to make it."

You often use food metaphors—"freedom tastes close to butter," "a whole new pie"—in your writing. What draws you to these culinary images and metaphors?
I love food.

I just went on this weeklong pie-eating road trip with one of my best friends, Angela. We called it the I Only Have Pies for You road trip. We tried pie all over the Midwest for a week, and I ended up writing about it.[2] I felt like that road trip became this microcosm of all that I stand for when it comes to food and just being *me*. The idea that, "Oh my God! Food can be this beautiful, shared experience that builds intimacy. Food can be this thing that creates embodiment." And then, also, there is something a bit controversial, a bit cheeky, about being a fat woman who is just like, "I refuse to accept your mandate that I eat vegetables in public or that I refuse to enjoy food." For me, there is definitely that campiness, that antiassimilation, where I'm like, "Oh, this is the thing that is going to make you uncomfortable, and I'm going to lean into that." So for sure there was a performative element to it, but there's also an educational or modeling element around showing other fat people that they deserve to have whatever relationship that they want to have with food. And if they want to have a joyful, bombastic, over-the-top, poetic relationship to food, they deserve to have that.

It's still really political as a fat person to eat in public and declare a love for food, because we've been taught that the reason we're fat is because we have this undisciplined, unacceptable relationship to food. There's often a lot of really delicious food at fat-activist gatherings. I've been talking with friends about this over time, and a lot of it has to do with the fact that we're trying to destigmatize the relationship to food that fat people have been taught. People have been very critical of the imagery around fat activism being cupcakes and donuts and whatnot. Even other fat people who are like, "Oh, you know, this is not promoting a complex portrayal of fatness or whatever. This is a parody." And I'm like, "You know, it is a parody." I think that that's okay, I think there is a little bit of an overcorrective component to it that is really valuable because of the level of stigma.

So at these gatherings we have all this food to convey that fat people deserve to eat a delicious thing as much as a thin person. You are not morally inferior because you are fat; you are not a failed thin person. When I was hating myself and restricting and dieting and all this stuff, I felt like I did not deserve to eat delicious things. That I would deserve to eat them later, when I was thin. Maybe, right? There's something really, really deep in that, because we know that these delicious foods bring extraordinary pleasure—the body is biologically wired to experience food as pleasurable. And the idea that diet culture comes in and interrupts and hijacks and ruins this amazing relationship that you can have in your body with food, with all the things around you, is just deplorable. It's completely immoral and it's completely unnatural. I like to assert my—and by extension, every fat person's—right to consume delicious things like butter and tiramisu or whatever.

I also find power in consistently articulating my love of food, because it was long a site of anxiety and shame and fear for me. I, as a fat woman, am not supposed to *love* delicious, rich foods, and I find power in refusing to acquiesce. And I love modeling to other fat people that they can have this really fun, joyful relationship to food and that they *deserve* that!

According to your writing and your Instagram feed, you're a pastry lover! What's your all-time favorite dessert?
It's a real toughie. For a long time, it was tiramisu. I do love crème brûlée. I guess I'd have to say... right now I'm obsessed with matcha. There's this matcha palace in Japantown in San Francisco. It's like the Church of Green Tea. They have a creamy matcha and a grassier matcha that is *like sldijflsdjflskjdlfj* (read: yum). And they have this thing called kakigōri—it's shaved ice with a hōjicha syrup topped with matcha soft serve topped with mochi balls and red beans and corn flakes, and you can add matcha powder. It's so deliciousss.

An earlier version of this interview was originally published as part of the Nourishing Resistance series at Bone + All.

Notes

1   George Monbiot, "Neoliberalism: The Ideology at the Root of All Our Problems," *Guardian*, April 15, 2016. https://www.theguardian.com/books/2016/apr/15/neoliberalism-ideology-problem-george-monbiot.

2   Virgie Tovar, "I Only Have Pies for You," *Medium*, October 13, 2019, https://medium.com/airbnbmag/pie-road-trip-56d196630956.

Everywhere That Feeling Lived: Making a Queer Food Podcast

Nico Wisler

I started thinking about the connections between my queer identity and food in 2016. Only nebulously. I happened to be visiting New York in June and was on the subway, scrolling through my phone, when I saw the news of the Pulse nightclub shooting. I was headed uptown for the Puerto Rican Day Parade but heard that folks were gathering downtown, in front of the Stonewall Inn. That a memorial was taking place. I stumbled off my train and across the platform. I wasn't the only one. All around me, would-be paradegoers in full gear—beads, face paint, flags, tank tops, and baseball hats, all emblazoned with the Puerto Rican flag—stood solemn-faced on the downtown train. The names of the Pulse victims hadn't been released yet, but already we knew that many of those killed had been Puerto Rican. In front of the bar, sitting in a vase among a sea of flowers and candles, were two small flags, the kind that look like they're attached to a chopstick: a pride flag and a Puerto Rican flag. I had never seen these flags next to each other. These two identities, both so core to how I understood myself, had always sat apart.

When I got back home to California, I couldn't sit down or keep my hands still. I went into the kitchen. I chopped peppers and garlic and herbs until my fingers were stained and cramped. I pulsed sofrito in batches in a food processor. I pulled out my big rice pot, the one I almost never use. And I texted every queer person I knew and asked them to come over the next evening, to eat and to grieve. When it was time to eat, we stuffed ourselves awkwardly into the kitchen. I had brought all of these people together—my closest friends, a handful of my exes, a bunch of strangers—but I wasn't sure what to say. Blessedly, just a day after the shooting, Justin Torres had written exactly the right thing, in an essay called "In Praise of Latin Night at the Queer Club." The opening lines had been rattling around in my head all day:

If you're lucky, they'll play some Latin cheese, that Aventura song from 15 years ago. If you're lucky, there will be drag queens and, if so, almost certainly they will be quick, razor-sharp with their humor, giving you the kind of performances that cut and heal all at once. If you're lucky, there will be go-go boys, every shade of brown.

Maybe your Ma blessed you on the way out the door. Maybe she wrapped a plate for you in the fridge so you don't come home and mess up her kitchen with your hunger.[1]

I couldn't stop thinking about those plates. How underneath the foil would probably be tostones, arroz con gandules, maybe a chuleta. Exactly what I'd made for my friends.

Here, still, it's hard to describe what the house felt like once I was done cooking and everyone had spread out. Every surface full of little clumps of queer people balancing plates on their knees. Some of them were openly weeping. Some of them were making out. Most were just talking quietly between bites. It's hard to describe what it feels like, really, every time I make food for queer people or eat something made by a queer person. A friend, a lover, a stranger, or a server who gives me a nod when they bring my plate.

Ever since that dinner, I've wanted to get everywhere that feeling lived, to talk about it with others who felt it, with those responsible for creating and sustaining it. In 2018, I reached out to the folks at Heritage Radio Network, a podcast station that hosts shows about food, and pitched a show called *Queer the Table*. Radio felt right for these stories because, like cooking, it's an intimate medium. It's sensory in a way that writing is not. It allows true space for breath or laughter or an outburst of shared understanding.

The conversations on *Queer the Table* often end up back at some version of that indescribable feeling. Queer food historian John Birdsall, Diaspora Co. founder Sana Javeri-Kadri, cookbook author Julia Turshen, and many others have all tried to name this something that is different about us and food. Something about what is centered in queer food business plans. Something about the way we grocery shop. Something about the way we read a menu. The way we farm. When we write a recipe down, or who it gets passed to. The way we share, the way we organize around food. The way it feels to cook for each other, to sit at a table with a family we chose.

Producing the show also uncovered for me ways in which my queer identity and my relationship to food were connected that I didn't necessarily expect. When I hosted that dinner party in 2016, I was just barely stepping to the other side of an eating disorder that had consumed my life for the better part of two years. I didn't know, at the time, that my obsession with restricting food and flattening my body had been about gender dysphoria. I didn't even really know what gender dysphoria was.

In 2019, when I was ready to make the episode that would come to be called "Changing Shape,"[2] I did know these things. I knew that I was going to make a piece about eating disorders and trans people and the ways in which treatment plans are by and large not designed for us. I knew all of this, and yet I still hadn't really moved past so much of what my treatment had taught me: that I needed to accept my body, as it was, to be healthy. Dr. Sand Chang, a psychologist I interviewed for the piece, was the person who told me that, actually, a study had come out showing that for trans people with eating disorders, the most effective treatment option was not, could not, be body acceptance. It was transition, surgical and/or social.

The tape is silent for a full five seconds as I process this information. I sit on it for a year. By the time I finally produce the episode, in the spring of 2020, with the tremendous support of the team at the podcast *Bodies*, I've had top surgery. I'm finally at home, truly, in my body. I'm ready to host brunches and barbecues and fancy dinner parties to celebrate with my friends. And a pandemic has just begun.

Over the last eighteen months, I have so, so rarely felt the feeling that drives *Queer the Table*. But it's still here. Early on in the pandemic, I was able to speak with activists at God's Love We Deliver and the Okra Project, two New York City–based organizations committed to keeping the most vulnerable among us well fed. They pivoted on a dime to socially distanced kitchens and contactless drop-off. The queer-owned cafe in my own neighborhood set up a community fridge around the same time.

It's still here. We're still here. I can't wait until we're around a table again.

Notes

1   Justin Torres, "In Praise of Latin Night at the Queer Club," *Washington Post*, June 13, 2016, https://www.washingtonpost.com/opinions/in-praise-of-latin-night-at-the-queer-club/2016/06/13/e841867e-317b-11e6-95c0-2a6873031302_story.html.

2   Nico Wisler, "Changing Shape," *Queer the Table*, Heritage Radio Network, September 3, 2020, podcast, 27:33, https://heritageradionetwork.org/podcast/changing-shape.

Queer Potlucks Offer Food for Capitalist Critique and Collective Action

Lindsey Danis

It's no surprise that previous generations of LGBTQ people found one another through food: in a world where queer sexuality was alternately closeted and coded, access granted through signals such as hankie flags or queer slang, LGBTQ people were hungry for connection. Being in community, taking care of one another, and serving as a surrogate family—those rejected by biological families reenact kinship structures in nonlinear, nonhierarchical ways. But running underneath queer potlucks, like the tofu used by broke lesbians to stretch a shared supper, are the seeds of self-actualization and anticapitalist action.

Despite notable exceptions (such as drag king and Stonewall activist Stormé DeLaverie), gay women tended to avoid the hypermasculine bar scene. They had less discretionary income than men and, if caught in a police bust, could lose custody of their children.[1] "There were places to go for entertainment and there was a certain ambiance, but there was not the sense of community that we have developed since," said Del Martin, cofounder of Daughters of Bilitis, the first lesbian-centered organization in the US.[2] Martin and her partner, Phyllis Lyon, attended a couples dinner for gay women in September 1955 in their North Beach, San Francisco, home, which seeded the lesbian organization. Daughters of Bilitis formed as a social outlet, with regular coffee hours called Gab 'n' Java, but soon became active in the nascent LGBTQ rights movement, which at the time focused on reducing stigma and trying to appease straight culture.[3]

As the women's sense of collective strength grew, so did their political consciousness. By the late 1960s, a new generation advocated for gay pride, equal pay, and abortion access.[4] While Black lesbians like DoB member Ernestine Eckstein saw the struggle for civil rights and LGBTQ rights as linked, the LGBTQ community wasn't always inclusive of Black women. Arguing that women couldn't achieve independence from men (and heterosexuality) without economic liberation, lesbians of color practiced intersectional activism, fighting for acceptance within the LGBTQ community and for higher wages for Black women, who had few opportunities to work outside the home. Sidelined within mainstream feminism and the DoB, these queer activists planned protests and fell in love around communal tables where tuna casseroles, lentil meatloafs, and tofu bakes were carefully planned in accordance with political boycotts.[5]

Vegetarian food was practical and poetic: lower salaries meant queer women often couldn't afford meat. At these informal gatherings, held in cheap shared apartments (these a precursor to the lesbian separatist farmsteads, communes, and queer house shares from the 1970s through present times), queer women questioned the patriarchal power structure that marginalized them. Rather than participate in the capitalist economy that prescribed their agency, the lesbians met group needs collectively, through an informal gift economy that stretched limited means.

Although the "crunchy granola" lesbian stereotype of the era turned into a meme to be laughed at by the next generation of radical dykes, these potlucks crystallized values of collective action and radical kinship that continue to guide queer community. To this day, LGBTQ folks provide shelter, care, and cash assistance to those who need aid, trusting that someone will help them in turn should they need it. These queer support networks take the place of the family support many LGBTQ folks were denied and operate outside of capitalism.

While lesbians are often written out of the queer community's response to AIDS, they delivered meals, organized blood drives, and donated blood when their male counterparts were (and continue to be) prohibited from donating.[6] Laura Stratton, who volunteered to deliver meals to AIDS patients in San Francisco, acknowledges the link between gendered socialization of women as nurturers and their care of AIDS patients, but also credits a community "affinity" between gay men and lesbians, as both were sidelined from cisgender, heterosexual culture.[7]

Caring for gay AIDS patients can be seen as an extension of gender-based nurturance conditioning, but there were practical considerations (lesbians were far less likely to get AIDS) and, as Jackie Winnow accounts in *Feminist Review*, caretaking gave queer women greater agency and visibility: "While there have always been unaddressed and painful divisions between lesbians and gay men, coming to the service of men around the issue of AIDS seemed finally to validate our existence."[8]

AIDS also mobilized the queer community to disrupt capitalism through direct action, such as the protests held by AIDS Coalition to Unleash Power (ACT UP). In interrupting pharmaceutical meetings or chaining themselves to politicians' desks, ACT UP members turned protests into public spectacles that gained media attention.[9] The protests were cathartic, but members also strategically capitalized on their exposure. When they were able to secure a meeting with FDA officials, they shared resources and eventually partnered with pharmaceutical researchers on AIDS research and treatment. The group's "inside-out strategy" deploys the logic of cooperation and exchange present in the potluck model. Queer activists recognized the harm caused by the pharmaceutical industry, but they worked to find common ground for mutual benefit, because the situation demanded it. ACT UP's partnership with the pharmaceutical industry hastened the discovery of the first AIDS cocktail, in 1996, says David France, author of *How to Survive a Plague*, a history of AIDS activism.[10] And the group modeled patient activism that's still used by chronically ill individuals, says France.

In present times, when LGBTQ people have greater (though not equal) rights, queer potlucks seem at first glance to provide emotional nurturance. Those held by SAGE, an organization that provides advocacy and services for LGBTQ elders, create spaces for multigenerational connection outside of the nuclear family structure.[11] For those rejected by biological families, this exchange can be healing. SAGE's gatherings also address the loneliness epidemic among LGBTQ older adults, three-quarters of whom expressed concern about having enough support from family and friends as they age, per a 2018 AARP study.[12]

In a SAGE potluck I attended in Red Hook, New York, students from the Culinary Institute of America made tacos for a rurally located audience of high school and college students, middle-aged adults, and older adults. Table seating was intergenerational, and icebreakers about queer history and personal life experience encouraged conversation. It was a safe environment for older adults to ask the younger generation about their experiences growing up in a more inclusive world and to have their experience as LGBTQ elders validated by the community.

Author Matt Ortile, a gay Filipino immigrant, describes the importance of such "chosen family" gatherings, not just among LGBTQ people but in other groups who "wade through trauma together": veterans, immigrants, and twelve-step communities. Writing about a communal dinner after the 2016 election, Ortile describes the power of coming together in times of crisis: "Meeting the group... for dinner, splitting bottles of wine. Holding hands, crying, laughing because we had to. I remember feeling helpless, outraged, but strangely, mercifully, as alienating as the election results were, not feeling alone."[13]

Post-2016, queer potlucks doubled as sites of resistance. Consider Queer Soup Night, Brooklyn-based chef and cookbook author Liz Alpern's "international community committed to resistance," which started in Brooklyn after the 2016 election and has eighteen affiliated chapters as of this writing.[14] While the soup initiative started in response to the 2016 election, Alpern's vision of activism, positive in nature and built to support those on the front lines, is forward-looking.

Queer Soup Night suppers are low-key affairs, designed to uplift attendees and gather resources (attendance is a ten-dollar suggested donation), which are passed on to nonprofits that strengthen local LGBTQ communities. Alpern tells *GO Magazine* that she saw a need for "queer folks and allies to gather in community and soak up the nourishment (physical and mental) we all need to keep doing the work we're doing while facing our harsh political climate," as well as for activism that is "joyful and constructive."[15]

While LGBTQ folks enjoy far greater rights than their ancestors, who could not openly love, there remains much work to be done, particularly in queer and trans BIPOC communities impacted by racial bias, health disparities, and unequal employment options, among other factors. As Ortile writes, "We must resist the American drive to prioritize nuclear families at the expense of the community and act instead in the spirit of kapwa, of radical togetherness with others."[16] Queer history offers examples of the forms this radical togetherness could take—sharing resources and shelter, disrupting politics for public health, and developing healthy alternatives to wounded family structures come to mind. In creating new narrative possibilities for their lives, LGBTQ activists have created broader societal change: first tolerance, then acceptance, and now allyship. To shift the needle further, queer people can draw on their rich cultural legacies to teach their allies how collective action and anticapitalist exchange models can address disparities.

Notes

1   Reina Gattuso, "How Lesbian Potlucks Nourished the LGBTQ Movement," *Atlas Obscura*, May 2, 2019, https://www.atlasobscura.com/articles/why-do-lesbians-have-potlucks-on-pride.

2   Zoe Martin, "Daughters of Bilitis: Historical Essay," FoundSF, published 2015, accessed December 30, 2020, https://www.foundsf.org/index.php?title=Daughters_of_Bilitis.

3   Gattuso, "How Lesbian Potlucks Nourished the LGBTQ Movement."

4   Gattuso, "How Lesbian Potlucks Nourished the LGBTQ Movement."

5   London Wages for Housework Committee, "International Lesbian Conference," *Power of Women: Magazine of the International Wages for Housework Campaign* no. 5 (1976), http://bcrw.barnard.edu/archive/lesbian.htm.

6   Jennifer Brier, "Locating Lesbian and Feminist Responses to AIDS, 1982–1984," *Women's Studies Quarterly* 35, no. 1/2 (2007): 234–48, http://www.jstor.org/stable/27649663.

7   Brittney McNamara, "Women Are Helping Fight AIDS during the AIDS/LifeCycle," *Teen Vogue*, June 4, 2017, https://www.teenvogue.com/story/women-help-fight-aids-aids-lifecycle.

8   Jackie Winnow, "Lesbians Evolving Health Care: Cancer and AIDS," *Feminist Review* no. 41 (Summer 1992): 68–76, https://doi.org/10.2307/1395233.

9   Nurith Aizenman, "How to Demand a Medical Breakthrough: Lessons from the AIDS Fight," February 9, 2019, on *Weekend Edition Saturday*, produced by NPR, transcript, https://www.npr.org/sections/health-shots/2019/02/09/689924838/how-to-demand-a-medical-breakthrough-lessons-from-the-aids-fight.

10 Aizenman, "How to Demand a Medical Breakthrough."

11 "Join SAGE Table," SAGE, accessed December 30, 2020, https://www.sageusa.org/join-sage-table/.

12 Angela Houghton, "Maintaining Dignity: A Survey of LGBT Adults Age 45 and Older," AARP, March 2018, https://www.aarp.org/research/topics/life/info-2018/maintaining-dignity-lgbt.html.

13 Matt Ortile, *The Groom Will Keep His Name* (New York: Bold Type Books, 2020), 262–65.

14 "Our Origin Story," Queer Soup Night, accessed December 30, 2020, https://www.queersoupnight.com/about.

15 Corinne Werder, "Seven Minutes in Heaven with Queer Soup Night Founder Liz Alpern," *GO Magazine*, January 2, 2018, http://gomag.com/article/seven-minutes-in-heaven-with-queer-soup-night-founder-liz-alpern/.

16 Ortile, *The Groom Will Keep His Name.*

The Hearth of Revolution

Shayontoni Rhea Ghosh

In the multipurpose living/dining/bedroom of my childhood home in Kolkata was a large wooden cabinet. It took up the entirety of one wall and housed the television, so a lot of our time was spent looking at it. Our clothes, my grandparents' documents, and assorted knickknacks were packed carefully in the dusty drawers. Right on top of the cabinet was a clunky black radio. The radio was always on. Our days—languid, humid, and melancholic—were set to a constant supporting soundtrack.

Today, my mother sings in the kitchen all the time. We're a territorial family and, while she will insist otherwise, Maa doesn't like sharing space in *her* kitchen. I stand at the door and watch her make aloo posto, a beloved Bengali dish. The poppy seeds are left to soak overnight and are ground with chilies to make a thick paste, which bathes cut potatoes and is cooked with nigella seeds, turmeric powder, and green chilies in mustard oil, then served with steamed ghee rice. Maa chats about the dish while making it, regaling me with stories about how Bengali people would, and still do, eat plates of rice and aloo posto for lunch and immediately treat themselves to a siesta.

My mother's ancestral home on her mother's side, in the Bikrampur jela of Dhaka, now Bangladesh, was, in her own words, heaven-sized. A sprawling property surrounded by fruit orchards, ponds, and farmlands, the house was a testament to the strength and community-oriented practices of the Bengali people. The orchard, in particular, stands out.

Colonial India was made up of war zones of numerous kinds. We were fighting the state, fighting amongst ourselves, bargaining with the forces of nature. We were watching familiar institutions crumble to dust and trying to rebuild. We were singing to keep our spirits up, dancing to retain agency over our mortal vessels, and walking, blindfolded, into a future we could not begin to map out.

In the first half of the twentieth century, resistance in the forms of the Swadeshi movement,[1] Gandhi's fervent attempts at nonviolence, and dissenting homebodies like young socialists, revolutionaries, political activists, and organizers were picking up steam. Skilled at dividing the community, the British government passed the Bengal Criminal Law Amendment Act of 1930[2] and instructed all local police stations to be on high alert for criminals and revolutionaries in their jurisdictions. Unexplained curfews, arbitrary arrests, and surprise home raids followed. The results of these were nothing to write to the British about—some "freedom-oriented literature" and a few stragglers. The local police, then, took a page from the colonizer's book and started considering divide-and-conquer strategies of their own. It was common for the police to pick up an innocent wage earner or a landless farmer, torture them with verbal and physical abuse, and release them on the condition that they become an informant. For the person in captivity, between a rock and the hard place of corrupt bureaucracy, the semblance of a choice was not apparent. Additionally, the police started to bribe the poor with pocket change and the promises of a better life if they could come to them with any incriminating information about their employers.

The home in Bikrampur sheltered many dissidents from the Dhaka Anushilan Samiti, the local branch of the revolutionary Anushilan Samiti movement.[3] Armed with the gift of space and the cover of nature, my great-grandfather Priyanath Ghoshal started building shacks in the orchard. Protected from the snooping eye by towering trees, the shacks would store mountains of dried leaves and branches by day and house dissenters on the run by night. Local organizers would stop him on the streets or in the market to ask for help, and one time he was approached by the devastated mother of a young revolutionary. His wife, my great-grandmother Kusumkumari Devi, was the only one who knew about the goings-on in the orchards. Terrified of the consequences but driven by principle, young Kusumkumari Devi took to the kitchen with vigor.

In *A Tale of Two Cities*, Charles Dickens wrote about "the vigorous tenacity of love, always so much stronger than hate." Was it love, then, that made my young great-grandmother cook for scores of unknown men and young boys? Tenacity that allowed my great-grandfather to shelter these headstrong and fiercely intelligent revolutionaries for days on end, risking the lives of his family and property? Perhaps. Today, as I gain a deeper understanding of the work I am here to serve—facilitating healing spaces for groups and individuals, creating theater, and writing—I tap into this quality of what-feels-like-love.

Kusumkumari Devi's kitchen was a space of devotion. Forced to cook for her guests by herself, and away from the hawklike gaze of their regular cook, she would let the silky masoor dal simmer while preparing baby potatoes in cumin seeds and mustard oil. She and her husband would carry the food out in batches into the orchard during the dead of night and keep watch while the revolutionaries gratefully wolfed everything down. Wary of informants, the young men were forced to leave every hideout spot after a week, at the latest. On the eve of their departure, my great-grandmother set about doing what she did best, scouring every market and every neighbor's home until she was able to collect a few pieces of fish. After thoroughly cleaning the fish and slathering them in turmeric, salt, and mustard oil, she set about cooking a simple curry to go with the ghee rice. That night the freedom fighters, persecuted by the state and the police, slept content.

My mother's father's ancestral home was in Ramna, Dhaka. My great-grandfather Monoranjan Chowdhury was not planning to house dissidents from the nearby localities, but when the door of his humble home shook with knocks in the middle of the night, he sprung to action. His wife, Hemprabha Devi, was resting after a long day of housework and childcare and was perturbed at the midnight interruption. However, when a group of fearful young boys poured into their home, she knew what needed to be done. She took to the kitchen immediately and soaked all the leftover rice from the day's meals in water. The next morning, when the sun's rays smiled over their home, the young couple served their guests a meal of paantabhaat—the soaked rice, served with a dash of oil, chilies, and some onions.

The following week was an exercise in self-restraint and generosity for my ancestors. I remain awed at the bravery they displayed in conversations with their neighbors, taking care never to reveal more than they should, always ensuring they weren't seen with more groceries than a household of three would need. The local police stations had already started plastering notices on public walls, asking citizens to step forward with any information about suspicious activities and strangers appearing in the neighborhoods. The air was heavy with fear.

My mother's father was four years old when the police barged into the house one night, demanding to know the whereabouts of a local youngster who was said to be helping the revolutionaries organize and find shelter. In the few seconds from the first knock on the door to the policemen entering the house, the dissidents had neatly packed themselves under the one bed of the house, holding in their breath and tears. Monoranjan Chowdhury shook in fake consternation and held down the fort while his wife, with my grandfather on her lap, demanded her house be emptied of the swine.

My ancestors shouldered immense risks in service of their faith and convictions. The slightest shift in energy or a step out of line could mean a few annas worth of information, and more than a few deaths. Today, when I consider the legacy of my ancestors, I see how tightly I am bound to their convictions. I'm committed to freedom from a fascist state, from spiritual and national terrorism. Freedom to dream, to thrive, and to hope for a softer tomorrow. I see the deep relevance of the kitchen as a gender-neutral and generative space of the home. A space of rebellion, communion, and awe.

Today, my mother protests as I elbow her out of the way and adamantly add a coat of olive oil to the potatoes. I grab the wooden spoon and stir the posto with determination. After spending a long time avoiding the kitchen and domestic duties, I am now opening up to the immense possibilities of creativity, collaboration, and freedom that emerge from a true connection with one's home, one's hearth. I feel the spirits of my great-grandmothers and grandmothers around me, watching with pride as I tighten my grip on the kadai and stir the chopped green chilies with the potatoes. My mother takes a minute to rest her feet as I start setting the table. Before the first bite, she closes her eyes and expresses gratitude for the food. Her face blossoms, and I experience a rush of indescribable emotion.

Our reverence practices ask us to dedicate food to our ancestors before eating. On some occasions, we prepare an entire plate that rests on the altar for a day. But, every day, we say their names in our minds before taking a bite. I remember my great-grandmothers, toiling over the fire, smoke in their eyes and hair, saris bunched up near their knees, and my great-grandfathers, bargaining at the markets, breaking their backs in the fields and at the factories. I remember the nameless, faceless ancestors who risked their lives in defense of life itself. I take a breath to return to the moment, and with love in my heart for who I am and what I serve, I take a bite.

It's always delicious.

Notes

1   "The Swadeshi Movement was the expression of the outrage triggered in Bengal by the partition of the province of Bengal in 1905. Though the colonial masters cited administrative reasons, the Bengalis were convinced that the Partition was a Machiavellian move to destroy the unity of the Bengali people, whose political activism the government had come to fear. The political message that the movement sent across was that if the British government refused to negotiate with their discontented subjects, they would be pressurized into doing so. It is within this context that we have to view the rise of the revolutionary nationalist movement that emerged as the most radical strand within the Swadeshi movement after 1907, with its claim that India had to become independent of British rule and if the British were not willing to grant independence to the Indians, then it had to be seized, by force if necessary. The immediate aim was to destabilise the British administration through acts of terror in preparation for the final revolution that would free India from colonial rule." Shukla Sanyal, "How the Revolutionary Nationalist Movement Gained Popularity in Bengal," *The Wire*, September 30, 2018, https://thewire.in/history/revolutionary-nationalist-movement-bengal.

2   "The Bengal Criminal Law Amendment Act, 1930," Bare Acts Live, accessed September 7, 2022, http://bareactslive.com/WB/WB239.HTM.

3   "The Anushilan Samiti was one of the premier organizations of the Indian revolutionaries which drew within its fold numerous brilliant revolutionaries and patriotic heroes who have left an indelible impression on the minds of the people and in the history of the Indian freedom movement. Founded in 1902, by Satish Chandra Bose with Barrister Pramanath Nath Mitra, it was wedded to the faith of emancipating the motherland through a nationwide armed revolt. The Anushilan Samiti made the British tremble and the latter had to acknowledge that it was one of the most powerful amongst revolutionary associations spreading from Bengal, Assam, Tippera, Bihar, Punjab, U.P., C.P. down to Poona. Its activities were married with strict secrecy. Its members received training in physical exercises playing with the lathi and the sword and also regular classes were held for its members in history, economics, political science and religion. It encouraged its members to undertake relief work among the common people in times of natural calamities with the object of coming into close contact with the masses. It developed a revolutionary press which issued newspapers, pamphlets and books preaching revolutionary activities including terrorism." Keka Datta Roy, "From Terrorism to Socialism: The Role of Anushilan Samiti (1935–47)," *Proceedings of the Indian History Congress* 69 (2008): 574–86, http://www.jstor.org/stable/44147221.

Rehearsing for Rebellion: On "Bella Ciao" and Italy's Radical Rice Weeders

Alessandra Bergamin

In the early spring, when the rice crops of the Po Valley—a fertile region of northern Italy fed by the country's longest river—were about two months old, thousands of women would leave behind their homes and families and travel by train, truck, or foot to labor in the flooded rice paddies. From around the seventeenth century until the 1960s, these women would arrive in towns such as Vercelli, Novara, and Cremona to work forty days each year as *mondine*, rice weeders. From dawn until dusk they stood in knee-deep water, plucking the weeds from the fledgling crops and stopping only to snack on meager rations. The crops had to be weeded multiple times throughout the growing process to prevent the young rice from being choked by other vegetation before it could be harvested. The flooded fields attracted malaria-carrying mosquitoes that stalked the women while they worked and as they retired to their threadbare dormitories. Conditions were so bad that in the early 1950s an Italian senator remarked, "Dante did not know the work of the rice weeders; if he did, he would have described it as a punishment in some circle of farmer hell."[1]

The mondine were not merely meek mothers, victims to an arduous job, however. The rice paddy was a red zone, a breeding ground of socialist, communist, and peasant-centered political ideology. At its center was a chorus of women, heads bowed and backs curved, harmonizing while they worked.

Through songs of resistance and revolution, the fields fostered radicalism. The older weeders would use the lyrics to teach the younger workers the history of protest, agitation, and activism, including that of the mondine themselves. "Bella Ciao" is perhaps their most famous song from the fields, though they are rarely acknowledged as its source. The lyrics describe a typical workday for the mondine as they leave their families to toil in the fields under the violent gaze of the foreman with his rod.

> *Alla mattina, appena alzata*
> *(coro) O bella ciao, bella ciao, bella ciao, ciao, ciao*
> *alla mattina appena alzata in risaia mi tocca andar.*
>
> *E tra gli insetti e le zanzare*
> *(coro) O bella ciao, bella ciao, bella ciao, ciao, ciao*
> *un duro lavoro mi tocca a far.*
>
> In the morning just got up
> (chorus) Oh bye beautiful, bye beautiful, bye beautiful, bye, bye,
> In the morning just awakened
> In the rice fields I must go.
>
> And among the insects and the mosquitoes
> (chorus) Oh bye beautiful, bye beautiful, bye beautiful, bye, bye,
> A difficult work I must do.[2]

In the decades since the mondine labored, "Bella Ciao" has been used in the Netflix show *Money Heist* and remixed, EDM-style, by DJ Steve Aoki. It has permeated Kurdish culture as a song of resistance. In Italy, the song has been used more recently to protest the xenophobic policies of the far-right political party Lega Nord (Northern League) and its member Matteo Salvini, who served as deputy prime minister. Amid the COVID-19 pandemic, "Bella Ciao" has had its latest resurgence. Videos have circulated showing Italians in Rome, Germans from the Bavarian town of Bamberg, and firefighters in the UK singing "Bella Ciao" from their balconies and rooftops and via YouTube. The Serbian National Theatre even recorded an orchestral version of "Bella Ciao" with each musician performing their part in isolation. The version sung today, however, is not that of the mondine. During World War II, "Bella Ciao" was adopted by the Italian partisans as an anti-Fascist song. The two songs share the same melody and refrain, but the lyrics have been altered to reflect their different oppressors: for the rice weeders it was the *padroni*, the foremen; for the partisans it was the Fascists. The origins of "Bella Ciao" are uncertain, but one version has been continuously remembered, adapted, and performed while the other has largely been written out of popular history, much like the legacy of the rice weeders themselves.

The Italian novelist Italo Calvino wrote, "Battles over the dignity of the Italian people have been fought in the rice fields."[3] In 1906, the town of Vercelli—located in the region of Piedmont, between Turin and Milan—was a site of one such battle. At the time, Italy had recently emerged from a period of repressive rule under King Umberto I, who was known to quash protests with violence, martial law, and restrictions on civil liberties. In 1900, he was assassinated by the Italian anarchist Gaetano Bresci, and Victor Emmanuel III became king. The new government favored constitutional rule, and trade unions across the country flourished. At the end of 1906, Italy's radical Socialist Party, to which many of the mondine had at least a loose affiliation, formed Italy's largest trade union, the General Italian Confederation of Labour (CGIL), which remains active today.

In May 1906, during the first days of the weeding season, the mondine began work stoppages with the ultimate goal of implementing an eight-hour workday. For decades, the rice weeders had worked in excess of ten hours per day. Because they were paid per day and overtime did not exist, their hourly wage kept decreasing. Forty years before, as malaria ran rampant through the fields, the Cantelli regulations of 1866—which prohibited work at dawn or after dusk, restricting possible work hours—was implemented to protect the weeding population. While the law was poorly enforced, it was something the mondine could build upon. As the historian Elda Gentili Zappi wrote in her book on the mondine, "The strikers marched from farm to farm carrying red and white banners, extolling the general strike, and singing the workers' anthem as well as a new song that was suddenly on the lips of all the weeders."[4] That song would later be known as "If Eight Hours Seem Too Few," and it describes the class struggle for an equitable working day.

> *Se otto ore sembran poche*
> *provate voi a lavorar*
> *e provarete la differenza*
> *di lavorare e di comandar*

> If eight hours seem few to you
> Try working

And you'll see the difference
Between work and giving orders[5]

While the strikes spread across the region, they were most explosive in Vercelli. In that city, alongside the mondine, others began demanding better hours and better pay, including metal workers, bakers, millers, gardeners, and women working in textile factories. One day in late May, the rice weeders intercepted people on their way to work, and they joined the strike; almost all of Vercelli shut down. In the following days, workers from all industries took over Piazza Torino, clashing with the troops sent in to disperse their protest and erecting barricades to prevent strikebreakers and the cavalry from entering the city. Eventually, the business owners conceded, prepared to resolve labor disputes if it meant that production would resume.

As a result of the mondine's organizing, bakers won the abolition of night work; metal workers, gardeners, and others won a shorter workday and better pay; and the rice weeders, as their song demanded, won the eight-hour workday by pushing the national government to draft a new bill on rice cultivation, which passed in 1907. But drastic labor changes are never easily implemented or retained, and the struggle did not end there for the mondine. Farmers, unhappy with the new legislation, sought out local lawmakers to help convince Prime Minister Giovanni Giolitti to repeal it. Giolitti decided to revoke the Cantelli regulations altogether, conceding to a growing conservative political climate. For the mondine, it took thousands more strikes and many more years to gain shorter work hours and higher pay. Their earliest foray into activism nonetheless set the tone for their future attempts to challenge the men in power and to struggle for a better working life through songs and strikes.

Given that the mondine were an all-female workforce, musical chorus, and activist group, it would be natural to suggest their political involvement was born of feminist ideas. But it is an anachronism to say they considered themselves feminists. The mondine saw their struggle as part of the international workers' rights movement they knew of through union involvement, socialist newspapers, and the songs sung in the fields and passed down generation to generation. It was only later, through oral histories and interviews that asked them to reflect upon their lives, that many rice weeders situated their politics within the broader feminist movement. Yet to be a woman in the rice fields was to experience work through a set of inherently gendered problems.

Malaria, miscarriage, and menstruation were as intertwined for the rice weeders as their bodies were with the act of labor. Among the mondine—who, contrary to the regulations, worked through dusk and dawn in the malarial rice swamps—it was estimated that for every thousand children born, six hundred died in their first year of life.[6] Complications such as premature birth and miscarriage were common, but the latter was not always unwelcome. Another baby meant another mouth to feed for an already impoverished family as well a momentary decline in income; pregnant women were forbidden by law from working in the rice fields. Writing about her mother's work as a mondina from the 1920s onward, writer Laura Scalabrini describes how the women would go to the fields at night to miscarry under the darkened sky. The fetuses would "fall on the naked earth, where they were hidden among dirt clumps with a piteous turn of the hoe and, often, with a profound sigh of relief for that suddenly interrupted pregnancy."[7]

It was common for middle- and upper-class women to stop working during menstruation even well into the 1940s. This was rarely an option for the low-income rice weeders, whose periods often ceased during the weeding season because their work was so physically taxing. For many, this pause in their cycle was a welcome relief; for those with unwanted pregnancies, there were other ways to move the process along. Diana Garvin, an assistant professor of Italian at the University of Oregon who has studied the mondine, writes that the rice weeders would jump off chairs, drink tisanes of parsley, and of course do their regular work in the fields to try to induce miscarriages. One rice weeder, pregnant with her fifth child, "hoped with all her might for a miscarriage" as she followed these folk traditions.[8] While she ended up carrying the fetus to term, the baby died within a few days of birth. There was a practicality to the rice weeders that did not necessarily hide their anguish or diminish their pain, but rather took into account what was realistic for a woman whose livelihood was wedded to her body.

From 1922 until World War II, during the height of Italian Fascism, Italy undertook an economic policy called the Battle for Grain. The aim of the propaganda campaign—which often portrayed Prime Minister Benito Mussolini bare-chested in Italy's grain fields—was to increase Italy's self-sufficiency by reducing the country's reliance on imported grain from Turkey. At the time, Italy's domestic grain production could not meet the nation's need for bread and pasta, so women, often families' sole cooks, were encouraged to increase their families' consumption of local staples such as rice instead. In the same period, Italy's birth rate was falling. The regime hoped to bolster the number of babies born in the Fascist state through government actions, including pamphlets on hygienic breastfeeding and tax incentives for families with children.

At the centers of both these policies were the women of the countryside, including the mondine. While the government dictated that a woman's place was at home, the very nature of Italy's plan for self-sufficiency required them to work in the fields. By 1922, only 5 to 20 percent of rice weeders were men, and women were paid around half as much for the same work. Propaganda portrayed these women as rustic and robust, maternal and working-class, celebrating them as "symbols of ideal Italian femininity," writes Garvin.[9] Yet even if the state wanted the bodies of rice weeders to be both bearers of children and laborers for the Fascists' purported greater good, the women themselves had other ideas.

From the 1920s onward, it was no secret that the majority of rice weeders voted for the Communist Party of Italy and carried in their wallets red voting cards symbolizing their resistance against the rising tide of Fascism. While Mussolini exalted the women as emblems of state-sanctioned motherhood, the rice weeders continued to use music in the fields as a rehearsal for rebellion. Throughout the Fascist period, even while other leftist groups were driven underground, the mondine staged strikes and protests, agitating for better hours, better pay, and better work conditions. They made considerable gains, too, such as improved food and shelter while they worked in the fields. The women's politics went beyond the personal. During Nazi occupation, writes Flora Derounian, a lecturer at the University of Sussex, many rice weeders left the fields and "refused to work for their oppressors," while others hid partisans in their homes and acted as couriers between battalions.[10]

During protests and strikes, especially in the Fascist era, the mondine were often arrested and targets of police violence. In the 2008 Italian documentary *Di Madre in Figlia (From Mother to Daughter)*, a former rice weeder recalls that she was so badly beaten by the police after a strike that she thought she would miscarry her unborn child. In 1949, Maria Margotti, a young widowed mother and staunch partisan, became one of the most famous martyrs of the Italian Resistance when she was killed by police during an agricultural protest in the town of Molinella. While Margotti died wearing a white scarf, often associated with the rice weeders, it is unclear whether she worked full-time in the rice fields. But her very public and very visible death at the hands of the government was representative of the assaults workers experienced each year in the "less visible space of the rice paddies," writes Laura E. Ruberto, a humanities professor at Berkeley City College.[11] In the days and decades since her murder, Margotti became not only a heroine of the mondine but was more broadly mythologized by the left as a symbol of Fascist resistance, peasant revolt, and, as a plaque erected in her memory in Molinella reads, a "companion of all the oppressed."

In the postwar years, when Italian neorealist cinema was at its height, Margotti, some have suggested, lived a visual afterlife through Silvana Mangano's character in the 1949 film *Bitter Rice*, directed by Giuseppe De Santis. The film, which was nominated for an Academy Award and competed at the Cannes Film Festival, thrust a glamorized version of the rice weeders onto an international stage. But this global fame was fleeting; soon after, the mondine, like so many women of history, returned to obscurity.

In the rice weeders' version of "Bella Ciao," the choir moves from speaking in the singular "I" to using the plural "us." It comes at the end of the song, when the women sing of a day when they "will work in liberty." This shift mirrors the way the mondine experienced a world where their burdens came not only from manual labor but from the triumph of capital over welfare, and their victories were won not only for the individual but for the greater collective. For the mondine—separated from their families, plagued by disease, and performing the kind of labor we would currently deem "essential"—hardship was not some great equalizer across gender and class but was instead a call to song, a cause of dissent, and a reason to reimagine what the world of workers, of peasants, and of women could look like.

"Rehearsing for Rebellion" was originally published in Lapham's Quarterly *on June 3, 2020.*

Notes

1   Flora Derounian, "Representations and Oral Histories of Working Women in Post–World War Two Italy (1945–1965)" (PhD diss., University of Bristol, 2018).

2   Translation by Diana Garvin, assistant professor of Italian at the University of Oregon. Diana Garvin, "Singing Truth to Power: Melodic Resistance and Bodily Revolt in Italy's Rice Fields," *Annali D'Italianistica* 34 (2016): 373–400, http://www.jstor.org/stable/26570497.

3   In 1950, Italo Calvino wrote about the mondine for the Italian Communist Party–funded publication *La Risaia*. Laura E. Ruberto, "Italian Rice Workers and National Popular Culture," in *Gramsci, Migration, and the Representation of Women's Work in Italy and the U.S.* (Lanham, MD: Lexington Books, 2010), 33–50.

4   Elda Gentili Zappi, *If Eight Hours Seem Too Few: Mobilization of Women Workers in the Italian Rice Fields* (Albany: State University of New York Press, 1991), 159.

5   Translation by Zappi, *If Eight Hours Seem Too Few*, 159.

6   Frank M. Snowden, *The Conquest of Malaria: Italy, 1900–1962* (New Haven, CT: Yale University Press, 2020), 109.

7   Garvin, "Singing Truth to Power," 386.

8   Garvin, "Singing Truth to Power," 387.

9   Garvin, "Singing Truth to Power," 380.

10   Flora Derounian, "How Women Rice Weeders in Italy Took on Fascism and Became Heroines of the Left," *The Conversation*, March 7, 2018, https://theconversation.com/how-women-rice-weeders-in-italy-took-on-fascism-and-became-heroines-of-the-left-92756.

11   Ruberto, "Italian Rice Workers and National Popular Culture," 33–50.

On the Food of the West Virginia Mine Wars

an interview with Mike Costello

Chef and journalist Mike Costello runs West Virginia's Lost Creek Farm with Amy Dawson and is the host and coproducer of the Pickle Shelf Radio Hour *podcast. In this interview, Costello talks about the role of food in the West Virginia Mine Wars, a series of union- and worker-led strikes that took place between 1912 and 1921. The Mine Wars included the Battle of Blair Mountain, the largest armed labor uprising in United States history, which was born out of the collaborative organizing of Black, Scots-Irish, and newly arrived immigrant Middle Eastern and European miners. Costello discusses the foodways of diverse mining communities, gardening as a way to sustain strikes, and how he sees one particular dish, chow chow, as emblematic of the inventive, community-focused cooking that typified the Mine Wars.*

Would you mind giving us a brief overview of the Mine Wars?
Yeah, of course. I should start by saying, I don't consider myself an expert necessarily, but I've learned a lot and have drawn a lot of inspiration from the Mine Wars over the years. And most of this I've learned through oral histories and by reading and digging for information on my own. I was still young, but this all came up years later than a lot of other state history I learned. There's so much great writing and research about the Mine Wars, but we're not exactly brought up to know about any of that here. In West Virginia, we take state-mandated history classes in fourth and eighth grades. But, you know, it's funny, even though the Mine Wars represent some of the most consequential moments of West Virginia history, it's not really something we're taught in school.

Back in 1912 was the first incident in what we think of as the West Virginia Mine Wars, and that was an organized mine strike at Paint Creek and Cabin Creek.[1] This was in the days when the coal industry was still somewhat fledgling but also rapidly expanding. There were a lot of miners who were fed up with poor wages and unsafe working conditions. Some of the conditions of working for the mining industry at the time were like, if you were going to buy anything, you were required to buy from the company store, for instance. It wasn't just that if you worked in the coal mines you were there for work—it was your community and your place in the community and your living situation and your shopping situation, and everything was determined by the company. And, of course, it was all to control the lives of the miners and their families.

I think it's important to put this into context and point out why this was the case. Around this time, the rest of the country was rapidly industrializing, the steel industry had taken off, the railroads were very productive, electricity was spreading to more and more places. So much of this industrialization depended on a steady flow of cheap coal. It was all touted as this great American prosperity, but it very much depended on that prosperity *not* being realized by working people in places like West Virginia. To have a steady supply of cheap coal, you have to have a couple of things in place, right? Of course, you have to have an abundance of the resource itself, which Appalachia had. But you also have to have a workforce that is easily controllable and willing to work under these conditions. We're talking many immigrants and a lot of people who are already in compromised economic circumstances. Otherwise, given an alternative, why would anyone choose to spend their days in such deadly workplaces, for little pay, to have every aspect of their lives controlled by the company?

So, the tensions would build, and, eventually, the miners started to work together in an attempt to unionize, to create leverage and organize against the mining company for higher wages, for better working conditions, and the removal of some of those stipulations, like the requirements to the company store. Of course, this was met with heavy resistance from the industry to the point that [coal companies] hired armed guards to push back against the miners with deadly force.

In my line of work, as a chef, educator, and a storyteller, I like to think about food narratives, whether we're talking about the Mine Wars or coal strikes in general or other labor struggles or anything else. Food is sort of the most universal means of survival, right? So, it's a great vehicle for telling stories about people. Given the history of West Virginia, the stories I tell are often about how people survived in the face of oppression under capitalism. That's the case in Appalachia or anywhere else where certain communities have been exploited, but narratives of place are often shaped by industries and governments. I like to use food as a way to tell a story we're not used to hearing. I talk about things a little bit differently depending on who the audience is. Sometimes I'll talk about what we can learn about ourselves because I'm talking to an audience inside of Appalachia or West Virginia. Then other times I'll be telling this story to people that are located outside the region who maybe have never been exposed to some of these bits of our history or some of the narratives around them. So that's a little bit of a side note in the overview of the Mine Wars, but I think it's an important one for the way I use food to tell stories.

Getting back to the Mine Wars, another incident of note that is probably more famous and notorious than the Cabin Creek and Paint Creek strike is the Battle of Blair Mountain,[2] which was also a struggle led by organized miners working basically for the same improvements in wages and conditions. It ended up with an armed struggle between those miners, armed guards from the companies, and then armed soldiers who represented the US government, which was fairly unprecedented. There was a lot of bloodshed in the mountains over that decade or so.

How is the story of the Mine Wars a food story?
That's a great question. And I guess to get people to connect something like the Mine Wars to food, I always like to think about this concept of survival. I mentioned earlier this sort of universality to seeing food as a means of survival. And that really helps us understand issues we don't think of as food issues or food stories in a different way. So, in West Virginia, the story of coal, at least as it's told by the industry or the state government, is also about survival. It's about us not being able to survive without the industry, right? As that story goes, without the industry, we would have nothing. I pointed out a couple of things we don't learn in school, but we make sure kids learn all the good things about coal,[3] how wonderful it is and how we couldn't possibly survive without it.

In all the situations of the Mine Wars and other strikes, you had miners in communities that were intentionally segregated. The companies knew that keeping miners separated, keeping them at odds with each other, made the workforce easier to control. They know that solidarity among workers would create power. They wanted to keep miners and their families segregated along lines of national origin, race, religion, and ethnicity. But if the miners could break down those barriers, they had some leverage. Together they had collective power that they didn't have when they remained confined by those walls of segregation. Miners were always under surveillance to make sure they weren't conversing, because in unity they were empowered.

A major way that sense of power was expressed was through the production and preservation of food. The miners' wives played a critical role in feeding striking miners and their families. These people typically didn't have access to much land for farming, or even large gardens, but families living in company houses, sometimes they had a small yard or a little bit of land that they could work with. Even a tiny garden really went a long way when you think about people working together and trying to feed each other. Like I mentioned earlier, these miners were required, as long as they worked for the mines, to buy from the company store. They didn't get paid in cash, so the company store was the only place where they could shop. Miners were paid in what was called scrip, and it was this company-specific currency that miners were paid in lieu of dollars. So, if they were on strike, they didn't have access to the company store and they had fewer options to feed themselves. The more food they could grow together, the more food they could preserve together, and that meant more power and leverage for striking miners. If they had more food on hand, they could extend the strike for longer. Otherwise, they had a harder time surviving in the coal camps and on the picket lines. Without food, there is no strike. Especially in the winter months, having food stores on hand meant striking or not, because when you're paid in scrip, you have no cash savings to spend elsewhere on food. Obviously, you have to eat to survive. So, the community that was created to grow and preserve food is a very significant, but often overlooked, part of our labor history.

It was remarkable for the time because there were a lot of Black miners moving up from the South during the Great Migration. Some of them had been sharecroppers and were expert farmers. You had these Eastern European miners, Irish miners that had expertise in agriculture that some of the Appalachian-born miners didn't necessarily have. As a lot of stories are told, they worked, by necessity, beyond these barriers of segregation to figure out where there were these complementary skill sets. They had to do this in secret, because the potential for unity was a threat to the coal industry, and, by extension, it was a threat to all of these other ancillary industries, and really to the national interest.

Multiracial working-class solidarity was a threat to industry profits, to widespread industrialization. It makes you realize how critical racism and white supremacy are to capitalism. If white workers and Black workers and Protestant workers and Catholic workers start to work with each other instead of against each other, it can spell trouble for the industry. The companies and even the government were prepared and willing to use deadly force to squelch these expressions of solidarity. So, when it came to Blair Mountain, that's exactly what happened.

In both my personal history and in my understanding of a broader Appalachian food history, I've always been drawn to these stories of people making food as a community. I mean, sometimes these concepts about "food and community" or "food bringing people together" are super cliché and downright myopic. But in rural places, there's a very real need to build community that's centered around food and justice, not because we want to feel good about ourselves, but because we just want to give ourselves the tools to survive. So, you look back and realize how difficult [it was] to overcome those barriers of segregation in those coal camps, and how powerful it was for that moment of solidarity to be realized and embraced and captured in such a way that we're still able to celebrate it today.

But at the same time, I think it's important to caution ourselves against reading too much into this as an antiracist history, or as racism somehow being eradicated from the picket lines. We know that, after the Mine Wars and after some mines were unionized, white supremacy flourished among these same miners, and there was rampant racism in the unions. It just sort of shows how, if it doesn't serve us, we can abandon white supremacy in order to achieve a specific goal. But we're so quick to sort of re-embrace it once it serves us again. I guess the message is that, of course, breaking down barriers during the Mine Wars is worth celebrating, but the need to work across these lines of segregation never stops if we truly expect to realize collective power.

Are there any specific dishes that are emblematic of or come from the Mine Wars era?
There are a lot of dishes that reflected this sort of Appalachian melting pot, because you had so many communities that were coming together at once. You had Italian miners, you had Hungarians and Black families, Syrians, Czechs, Russians, and so on. When you look back to the history

of Appalachian food, there were all these really proud food traditions that these people brought with them that shapes how and what we eat today.

Not all of [the traditions] they could really keep alive, because let's take, for instance, immigrants from Greece or Italy or elsewhere in southern Europe: they didn't have access to a lot of familiar ingredients [in Appalachia]. But all over West Virginia, not just in the coalfields, there are a couple of traditions that tended to take root more so than others. Those were typically meat preservation, because you can do that with salt, maybe some spices. There's canning of certain things like chow chow or these Italian-style peppers that people still make a lot of in the community where I live now. Breads and pastries were big, too, because you could still access, for the most part, the staples like flour, salt, and sugar, which is all you really needed for those things.

I haven't seen much of a detailed account of exactly what families were eating during the Mine Wars, but because we know a lot about the ethnic groups that made up the coalfields, and we know a fair amount about the food traditions of those communities, we can speculate. I often like to talk about foods like chow chow and pickles and whatnot because the idea of these small gardens that people were using to grow and preserve food together—you know, it's so symbolic of the way that people went to great lengths to work together.

The garden is just so significant because, again, food equals power. And when your food supply determines your power, the garden becomes a weapon. Everybody knew that the garden was a weapon, and the miners' wives especially used that weapon to strengthen the power of striking miners. The coal companies knew this, too. When coal bosses realized these gardens could be used as weapons against them, they would send their thugs out and they would destroy gardens. When people started growing and preserving food together, [the companies] knew that it created a situation where the miners and their families would no longer have to rely as much on the company and the company store. I think it illustrates how there's so much power in our food. It can be weaponized so easily.

When I think about this, the other part of this country's history that comes to mind is the buffalo being nearly extirpated during the imperialist expansion westward and into the Great Plains. Sometimes we hear, "Oh, you know, the buffalo were nearly hunted to extinction," which is complete nonsense. As a critical food supply for many Native cultures, the buffalo were slaughtered in unfathomable numbers intentionally. Native crops were destroyed for the same reasons. Controlling food supplies has been a tool used by oppressors throughout history.

So, in the coalfields, everybody in those camps knew that there was so much power in the garden, just as much as there were powers found in their guns and their bullets. We don't often think of food like this, but there was so much power in the small things like the peppers and the turnips and the tomatoes that make up dishes like chow chow. So, I kind of use chow chow as a symbolic dish to tell a story that goes well beyond food.

Can you tell us more about chow chow?
There's some variation of this dish—it's a pretty basic pickled relish made of a bunch of different vegetables—in so many cultures that have a history of growing and preserving food. And in the coalfields, that was just about every culture, right? So, basically, chow chow is a hodgepodge of whatever is left in the garden at the end of the growing season. Let's say I'm growing cabbage, tomatoes, corn, and peppers. At the end of the harvest season, maybe I'll make lots of kraut with my cabbage. I'll sauce the tomatoes, pickle the peppers, and I'll make a big batch of canned corn. But for each of those crops I'll probably have a little bit left over. Not enough to make another whole batch of something, but definitely enough to combine with those other things to make something else. So, I could take that cabbage, corn, the peppers and tomatoes, chop them all up, season them, and preserve them as this nourishing, flavorful relish. It's really beautiful. It's bright and tangy, and it could be totally different every time you make it, because you make it according to what's available. Sometimes there are beans in the recipe; sometimes it's almost all green tomatoes. It really just depends. I mostly know of that pickled relish as something commonly called chow chow, but there are a million names for it, and even among recipes for chow chow, there can be so many differences.

For me, again, it's kind of a symbolic dish. It represents a lot of themes I associate with Appalachian cuisine, but it's not just Appalachian. Because some variation of this is found all over the world, it's so easy to imagine jars of similar foods being packed and put away in the pantry by all these different families during the Mine Wars. Some of the recipes I have are called vinegar relish, Spanish relish, pepper and cabbage relish, and even mango relish. (Mango was a nickname for bell peppers in the early twentieth century.) But if you look at the recipes, we're talking about the exact same thing.

With chow chow or these other relishes, I think about the Mine Wars a lot, and I think about families with small gardens beside their company houses. You know, maybe they're only able to contribute a little bit from the garden to this overall goal of community food preservation. But that's the whole concept of chow chow: a little bit goes a long way, especially in tandem with all these other vegetables. There's this deep parallel that's always on my mind. I mean, imagine what makes up a jar of chow chow. In very small quantities, those ingredients have limited power on their own, but look at what happens when they work together. There's a community at work inside that jar. And together, that community creates something beautiful and so unique and delicious. In a way, it highlights the importance of solidarity and provides these lessons we can apply on a human level. Sometimes I say this and people think this is so esoteric or far-fetched, and to me that's just because we've let our storytelling traditions slip away. I don't tell these stories as a historian, presenting fact-based accounts of people's eating habits during the Mine Wars. I use something like chow chow as a symbol, as a vehicle for a narrative I think is inspiring. And ultimately, I guess the story of the Mine Wars itself is also symbolic, something I hope people can learn from and apply to their thinking moving forward. We can derive a lot of inspiration from stories that connect food to people and places and historical events, and those stories are an important part of keeping food culture alive. When we see food as this kind of empty thing that gives us calories and, sure, maybe some enjoyment from flavors, it's something we can enjoy and even love with a lot of passion. But it's not the same as seeing it as part of your culture. I think most of us can probably think of foods we love, not because of the actual flavors or ingredients, but because of the people or the places or times in our lives we associate those foods with. That's all storytelling. It takes stories about how these foods matter to us as people that make them part of our culture—a living, breathing thing we're more inspired to preserve.

The erosion of, or at least the manipulation of, food storytelling is also another tactic of controlling what we eat under capitalism. We're constantly fed stories through advertising and readily believe so many narratives that are presented to us about what certain foods represent, especially around class and economic status. For instance, in the early to mid 1900s, there were entire class-centric marketing campaigns for things like Wonder Bread or Jell-O and all of these other processed and packaged foods. These were often about status and shame. I remember some ads that were like, "Don't get caught sending your kid to school with that bread you make at home." You know, like, "How embarrassing that would be for you if everyone found out you're unable to buy bread from the store. Choose Wonder Bread so you can show off your status." I'm paraphrasing, but that's essentially the message. Maybe Wonder Bread didn't have company thugs going out and destroying home bakers' flour supply like the coal companies were doing to backyard gardens, but through these stories, they're still removing tools of self-sufficiency to create dependence on companies.

So, this leads me back to something like chow chow and the baggage that exists when we frame certain dishes as foods people ate not because they wanted to, but because they had to. And because of that story, I see a lot of folks running away from these particular food traditions. Americans have this tendency to stigmatize poverty, to make it seem like a result of personal failure, not a result of the awful systems and conditions of exploitative capitalism. So, if chow chow is associated with hard times and necessity, some people will see a story of failure. And they don't want to see that failure, so they run away from it. You know, they don't want to be associated with the *kinds* of people who have to eat chow chow. Just another parallel is that during the Mine Wars, striking miners and their families were portrayed as those same kinds of people: lazy, backward, helpless people who are in these tough situations, not because of the system, but because they've done it to themselves.

And when we talk about food, we don't really do a good job of countering those narratives by connecting food stories back to things we might be inspired by, whether that's our own struggles for justice or anything else. We're still conditioned to run away from what we perceive to be narratives of shame, so we don't often make a case that in something like a jar of chow chow is a narrative of something worth celebrating. But to me, chow chow is about complexity and the incredibly impressive outcomes that exist when these ingredients work together. So, I guess, flipping some of those narratives and transforming them into something that gives us inspiration and strength is empowering, really. At least that's what I hope to achieve. It definitely keeps me going.

How do you see the food narratives of the Mine Wars showing up today?

You know, I look back on those moments when I learned about the Mine Wars, in high school, then more so in college. It's funny to me now how shocked or surprised I was to learn about certain aspects of this conflict. You know, we tend to have these reactions to certain things we learn about at first. It's like, "Oh, wow, how could we *not* have learned about this in school?" But the more you pay attention and contextualize something like the Mine Wars by what's happening in the present day, the more it makes sense, right? Why *would* the state teach us this?

So, I guess I don't *just* think about the food narratives, but right now I'm thinking a lot about the food industry of today as a parallel to the coal industry of the early 1900s. For instance, commercial poultry has a huge industrial footprint in West Virginia. And in West Virginia and plenty of other places, we can take one look at that industry and see some of the same things happening. Okay, so there's a largely migrant workforce—people from many countries, of several religions, speaking many different languages. The wages are abysmal. The working conditions are unsafe, often deadly. It all sounds pretty familiar, especially when you ask yourself, what happens when these workers speak up? Well, as we've seen by now, the federal government comes in and arrests workers and their families, and that often leads to deportation. It's terrorism, just as it was on Blair Mountain. That's not a stretch, right? How many ICE raids have we heard about in poultry-processing communities over the past few years? Quite a few. People in these situations risk so much just by speaking up. It's very coercive. Fundamentally, it's a similar dynamic to the federal government sending troops to kill workers at Blair Mountain after they stood up for fair wages and safer conditions. When you take steps to loosen the grip of capitalism, you quite literally become an enemy of the state.

Growing up here, you learn how far the state will go to protect industry, to demonize people who speak out or threaten industry's position. Not only does the history start to make so much sense, but you see that history repeating itself in so many ways. Again and again, it always repeats. So, the need to tell our stories never ends.

An earlier version of this interview was originally published as part of the Nourishing Resistance series at Bone + All.

Notes

1   "Paint Creek and Cabin Creek Strikes," National Park Service, accessed August 10, 2021, https://www.nps.gov/articles/000/paint-creek-and-cabin-creek-strikes.htm.

2   "The Battle of Blair Mountain," National Park Service, accessed August 10, 2021, https://www.nps.gov/articles/000/the-battle-of-blair-mountain.htm.

3   Jackie Ayres, "Coal in the Classroom," *Register-Herald*, updated July 29, 2014, https://www.register-herald.com/news/local_news/coal-in-the-classroom/article_233db751-3bd4-57cb-83ef-6d495a036a22.html.

Notes on Utopian Failure in the Commune Kitchens

Madeline Lane-McKinley

> *...failure*
> *to believe the dictionary & that there is anything*
> *to teach; failure*
> *to teach properly; failure*
> *to believe in teaching*
> *to just think that everybody knows everything*
> *which is not my failure; I know everyone does; failure*
> *to see not everyone believes this knowing and*
> *to think we cannot last till the success of knowing*
> *to wash all the dishes only takes ten minutes*
> *to write a thousand poems in an hour*
> *to do an epic, open the unwashed window*
> *to let in you know who and*
> *to spirit thoughts and poems away from concerns*
> *to just let us know, we will*
> *to paint your ceilings & walls for free*
> —Bernadette Mayer, "Failures in Infinitives"[1]

Of her time living in a twelve-person commune in 1969, Kit Leder recalls a rude awakening. "Women did most of the cooking, all of the cleaning up, and, of course, the washing," she tells communalist historian Timothy Miller. "They also worked in the fields all day, so that after the farm work was finished, the men could be found sitting around talking and taking naps while the women prepared supper." Looking back on her experiences as a communard, Leder describes with disappointment the way this "well-known pattern emerged immediately"—"even though," as she explains, "there was no society-dictated division of labor, even though we had complete freedom to determine the division of labor ourselves."[2]

Throughout so many accounts of the "hip communes" of the long Sixties, this conflict is abundantly clear yet hardly mentioned. In journalist Richard Fairfield's 1972 travelogue, *Communes USA: A Personal Tour*, an exhaustive overview of some of the more prominent communes, the misogyny is rampant. "It's really unbelievable what those chicks have learned to do over a fire that's nothing more than a hole in the ground," an unnamed male "leader" explains to Fairfield of his commune. "If the chicks aren't making it, if the chicks don't have any energy and don't want to do anything, like be chicks, you know, wash dishes, cook, then you're in for trouble."[3] Women who had left for the communes to reject a traditional life, in a variety of forms, found themselves profoundly trapped.

According to sociologist Benjamin Zablocki, who spent years researching the New Communalist phenomenon across the United States, women in the communes spent more than double the amount of time men did on cleaning, cooking, and dish washing. "The rationale for sexual freedom is that it provides liberation," writes Zablocki. "Yet the evidence that we have seen suggests that such liberation has not happened either in the domain of work or in the domain of relationships." Out of all the communes he studied, Zablocki concluded that no commune was able to overcome this division, though some made substantial efforts. "In some communes some of the women came to be defined as either mothers or females, but not both," he elaborates.[4] One of the women interviewed in his study complained that she had to keep leaving different communes because of the way that "free love" was enforced by a patriarchal power structure. At one of the communes, she found herself the last remaining "female" and escaped the mandate to be "free, loose, and sexually available" at all times.[5] Meanwhile, the "mothers" had become overwhelmed with the meal preparation, dish washing, and laundry.

Of her years traveling between different communes, Vivian Estellachild recalls how communal living appeared to her as a "step in the right direction," followed by the painful discovery that most communes were using "women in a group way the same as the fathers did in a one-to-one way."[6] For many, the heartbreak was too great.

Between 1963 and 1975, there were thousands of communes proliferating around the United States in all regions. At the peak of New Communalism, there were over a million people living collectively off-grid, dropping out from the world of careers, education, and the nuclear family. Yet while communalism and communalist practices proliferated, the average commune lasted no more than nine months, disbanding for a variety of typical reasons: lack of infrastructure, unsustainable resources, political targeting, and, of course, internal conflict. A particular "brand of kaleido-scopic ruin" is not uncommon to this history, as author and curator Erin Elder writes of the communes that spread across the Southwest. As Elder speculates, this kaleidoscopic vision of the communes possibly accounts for "the ways in which their legacy has been ignored or oversimplified."[7]

A key example of this communal ruin is Drop City, once located outside of Trinidad, Colorado. One of the more notorious communes at the time, Drop City was established by art students Clark Richert and Gene and Joann Bernofsky in May 1965. Inspired by the architectural designs of Buckminster Fuller and Steve Baer, the Droppers created a total of seventeen inhabitable dome structures, repurposing trash and scraps from junkyards. In images and film footage of the commune, Drop City appears as if a cosmic imaginary had dropped onto a stark prairie land-scape. Conceptually, Drop City embodies many of the utopian dimensions of New Communalism, as a site of dropping out and radical departure, but also of speculative futurity and worlding. The Droppers had an open-door policy, inviting anyone to participate in what Alastair Gordon, another ethnographer of the communes, described at the time as "an ongoing collaborative performance [of] living spontaneously and intuitively," in which "art, life, and politics [merged] into an all-for-one web of synergy." Eventually, however, Drop City turned into what communalist scholar Robert P. Sutton characterizes as a "communal slum":

> The garden started by the first Droppers became an arid patch of pigweed. There were no work assignments, so all tasks were done voluntarily, most not at all.... The kitchen, [ransacked], was infested with transients. There was not enough money to purchase soap, and everyone was filthy. Food stamps lasted only halfway through the month and then they went to Trinidad to scavenge food from outdoor trash containers. The single outhouse overflowed and there was no lime to clean it. Hepatitis spread through the colony. They stopped admitting visitors.[8]

Before the commune was shut down by the local health department in 1973, there were rumors of a methamphetamine factory and a murder, along with a round of hepatitis.[9]

Tales of ransacked kitchens and overflowing outhouses can be traced throughout the history of New Communalism and its case studies of communal life. For the communes that miraculously survived the end of the Sixties, as it stretched into the capitalist recuperationism of the mid-Seventies, the story was not of degeneration but mutation. Among the longer-lasting communes, many transformed into bed-and-break-fasts, industrial farms, or nonprofit organizations. The alternative to giving up on the dream, in other words, was compromising the dream— or at least, that's how the story often goes.

Yet the politics of this story are also quite familiar: that of utopianism as either foolish or dangerous and, regardless, doomed to failure.

By the mid-Seventies—what would be the last gasp of New Communalism—kitchens were battlegrounds for feminist critique and counterinsurgencies in the communes. Women from different communes were coming together to share their experiences and experiment with ways to collectivize within and across communes. In 1974, in an anonymous editorial for the communalist publication *Communities*, women from different communes compared their struggles and collectively authored an analysis of patriarchal dynamics in the communes. Based on their experiences, the authors agreed that, "especially for women who are coming from nuclear family situations," including many contexts of domestic violence and sexual abuse, "the freedom of communal living is immensely rewarding on a very practical level." However, as they explain, "work in the communes other than the necessary everyday chores often still reflects the conditioning we have all gone through."[10]

These critical interventions within New Communalism reflect an accelerated version of what Silvia Federici and Nicole Cox, major figures in the Wages for Housework movement at the time, conceived as "counterplanning from the kitchen": a practice of transforming the atomization of housework into a collective struggle. At a formal level, the communal kitchens overcame many obstacles faced by women in their everyday lives. While a gendered division of labor still materialized, it was different from the context of the working-class household in which, as Federici and Cox explain, "trying to educate men always meant once again that our struggle was privatized and fought in the solitude of our kitchens and bedrooms."[11] In the communes, women were not isolated in the kitchens, but collectively galvanized. Instead of solitude, the communalist kitchen became a site of commiseration—and sabotage. Women were banding together, building strategies to transform and denaturalize the division of labor among communards, and finding ways to reimagine their dreams for communalism together.

This counterplanning strikes an important contrast with the "tyranny of structurelessness" that Jo Freeman describes of the Women's Liberation movement by the end of the Sixties. In her 1971 essay, Freeman warns against anarchist tendencies emerging among feminists: a "hegemony [that] can be so easily established because the idea of 'structurelessness' does not prevent the formation of informal structures, only formal ones."[12] The slow creep of patriarchal control experienced across the communes was facilitated by this utopianism of structurelessness in many ways: it enabled chauvinism and coercion through informal structures of power, which were easily denied or disputed by the ambiance of leaderless egalitarianism. Yet what gets missed in this denunciation is the way in which contradictions provoked confrontation, struggle, and collective inquiry.

Freeman's critique of "structurelessness" is consistent with the "fairly stable set of indictments" in liberalism's case against utopia, which Kathi Weeks describes as historically vacillating between rationalist and realist rebukes—"the claim that there should be no alternative," writes Weeks, "and the assurance that there is no alternative."[13] With the charge of "tyranny," Freeman invokes Karl Popper's antiutopianism: "The Utopian attempt to realize an ideal state, using a blueprint of society as a whole," Popper asserts, "demands a strong centralized rule of a few, [and therefore] is likely to lead to a dictatorship."[14] Popper's denunciations of this "Utopian attempt" fail to develop a critique of the attempt itself, engaging with utopia as a blueprint or program but never as an epistemology or method.

Rather than structurelessness, what I am describing here as a kitchen-based utopianism might be better understood as a practice of *communitas*. On the one hand, the division of labor that took hold of most communes was thoroughly dystopian—a dream that contorted, rapidly, into a nightmare. On the other hand, the practices that emerged from this nightmare provide a basis for "a kind of utopia," as Ursula K. Le Guin writes, which comes out of "margins, negations, and obscurities."[15] Drawing from anthropologist Victor Turner, Le Guin explains that "structure provides a model, *communitas* a potential."[16] This potential is grasped at, however briefly, through experimentation, reflection, and care. For Le Guin, *communitas* makes possible a "non-Euclidean," unmappable utopianism, which rejects the utopianism of "models, plans, blueprints, wiring diagrams" and which cannot be found by going forward, "but only roundabout or sideways," defiant of "tyranny."

Failure, as utopian theorist Ruth Levitas argues, is an "inevitable part of the process of trying to think utopia itself." In the hip communes, a kitchen-based utopianism was never part of the plan, and in many ways, it was out of the failure of plans and planning that this utopianism began to cultivate. It was a utopianism not premised on perfection, or the avoidance of failure, but on experimentation and working through failure. It is a utopianism for which there is much to learn from cooking—what brought the women together in the kitchen, teaching each other and discovering how to make the best loaf of bread or a soup to feed the most people based on the fewest ingredients, discussing mistakes, and observing each other's different styles and techniques.

Straying from the engineering metaphors, Marx's refusal to write "recipes for the kitchens of the future"[17] provides an essential critique of blueprintism, but not a theory of recipes. Whereas the blueprint is oriented toward finality and closure, the recipe takes its orientation toward repetition, adaptation, and transformation. A recipe means very little, that is, without a practice to explore it. And out of failure comes a deeper sense of method. As a set of instructions, recipes provide a basis for improvisation.

To learn from a recipe means applying it to different contexts, changing the ingredients based on availability, and reinterpreting the instructions for new purposes—and, sometimes, this means failing. Writing of cooking as an everyday practice, Luce Giard suggests that "to the extent that experience is acquired, style affirms itself, taste distinguishes itself, imagination frees itself, and the recipe itself loses significance." Losing its significance, the recipe becomes "little more than an occasion for a free invention by analogy or association of ideas, through a subtle game of substitutions, abandonments, additions, and borrowings." When given the same recipe, "two experienced cooks will obtain different results because other elements intervene in the preparation: a personal touch, the knowledge or ignorance of tiny secret practices." There is, as Girard elaborates, "an entire relationship to things that the recipe does not codify and hardly clarifies."[18]

To understand "utopia" for its design—and, therein, its failures—is to mistake a recipe for the meal itself.

Notes

1   Bernadette Mayer, "Failures in Infinitives," in *A Bernadette Mayer Reader* (New York: New Directions, 1992), 139.

2   Timothy Miller, *The 60s Communes: Hippies and Beyond* (Syracuse, NY: Syracuse University Press, 1999), 81.

3   Richard Fairfield, *Communes USA: A Personal Tour* (Baltimore: Penguin Press, 1973), 107.

4   Benjamin Zablocki, *Alienation and Charisma: A Study of Contemporary American Communes* (London: Free Press, 1980), 343.

5   Zablocki, *Alienation and Charisma*, 34.

6   John Anthony Moretta, *The Hippies: A 1960s History* (Jefferson, NC: McFarland, 2017), 252.

7   Erin Elder, "How to Build a Commune: Drop City's Influence on the Southwestern Commune Movement," in *West of Center: Art and the Counterculture Experiment in America, 1965–1977*, ed. Elissa Auther and Adam Lerner (Minneapolis: University of Minnesota Press, 2012), 20.

8   Robert P. Sutton, *Communal Utopias and the American Experience: Secular Communities, 1824–2000* (Westport, CT: Greenwood Publishing Group, 2004), 136.

9   Elder, "How to Build a Commune," 23.

10 Communities Collective, "Some Views from Women in the Communes," *Communities* no. 7 (1974).

11 Silvia Federici and Nicole Cox, "Counter-Planning from the Kitchen," in *Revolution at Point Zero: Housework, Reproduction, and Feminist Struggle* (Oakland: PM Press, 2012), 29.

12 Jo Freeman, "The Tyranny of Structurelessness," in *Revolutionary Feminism*, vol. 3 of the Communist Intervention Series (n.p.: Communist Research Cluster, 2015), 158.

13 Kathi Weeks, *The Problem with Work: Feminism, Marxism, Antiwork Politics, and Postwork Imaginaries* (Durham, NC: Duke University Press, 2011), 181.

14 Karl Popper, *The Open Society and Its Enemies* (London: Routledge, 2012), 149.

15 Ursula K. Le Guin, "A Non-Euclidean View of California as a Cold Place to Be," in *Dancing at the Edge of the World: Thoughts on Words, Women, Places* (New York: Grove Press, 1997), 88.

16 Le Guin, "A Non-Euclidean View of California as a Cold Place to Be," 96.

17 This passage has been retranslated several ways from Marx's 1873 afterword to the Economic Manuscripts of *Capital*, vol. I. See discussion of varied translations and interpretations in Terence Bell, "History: Critique and Irony," in *The Cambridge Companion to Marx*, ed. Terrell Carver (Cambridge, UK: Cambridge University Press, 1991), 139.

18 Luce Giard with Michel de Certeau and Pierre Mayol, *The Practice of Everyday Life*, vol. 2, *Living and Cooking*, 2nd ed., trans. Timothy J. Tomasik (Minneapolis: University of Minnesota Press, 1998), 201.

Abundance and Other Lessons on the Lower East Side

Wren Awry

The stairwell that led to ABC No Rio's second-floor kitchen was dim and dusty, and as I made my way up it, my high-tops kicked at painted plaster fallen from the mural-covered walls. But at the top of the stairs, sunlight streamed through the kitchen window and illuminated the landing. My friend Sebastian and I stepped across the threshold and into the kitchen, where a table piled high with dumpster-dived vegetables and donated bags of bread was surrounded by a half-dozen volunteers. The year was 2006 and we were both seventeen years old, two kids who attended Catholic school in the nearby suburbs and took the train to the city on the weekends to go to punk shows and protests. We volunteered with Manhattan Food Not Bombs at ABC No Rio—a radical social center housed in a Lower East Side tenement from 1980 to 2016—every other Sunday throughout that school year.

"Mold is usually fine to just cut off," the thirty-something punk who bottom-lined the free meal, served each week in nearby Tompkins Square Park, told us the first time we volunteered. "But some people are allergic to it and we won't know, so compost the whole thing," she added. She picked up a tomato flecked with fuzzy green and held it out to us as an example before adding it to a bowl of scraps, which would ultimately be turned into a rich humus to coax flowers, peppers, and herbs out of the soil at one of the nearby community gardens. She showed us how to rinse off vegetables in a bowl of cold water and brush away lodged dirt, then pointed us to a pile of knives and cutting boards.

As we peeled and diced, the other volunteers told stories. Most of them were five to fifteen years older than Sebastian and me. They talked about where they lived across the river in Brooklyn, in squatted buildings with fantastic names like the Batcave, and reminisced about the 2004 Republican National Convention (RNC): some rode as part of the six-thousand-strong Critical Mass bike ride, while others were part of a lawsuit that wouldn't be won until 2014, seeking amends for the hundreds of RNC protesters held at a bus-depot-turned-holding-facility without processing for over twenty-four hours. They also spoke of the fight to save the Lower East Side's community gardens, which was ongoing but had come to a pitch a few years earlier, at the turn of the millennium. Then, coalitions occupied and defended spaces like Jardín de la Esperanza on East Seventh Street, where they locked down inside a giant coquí in an attempt to stop bulldozers from knocking down vegetable patches, grapevines, and the garden's casita.

Years later, I became interested in stories of food-related mutual aid—reciprocal community care that prioritizes solidarity over charity and is often eclipsed by the equally necessary but more pointedly disruptive work of street protests and direct actions. As I dug into the topic, I realized that the Lower East Side teemed with histories of radical food sharing and places where growing and preparing meals intertwined with resistance to capitalism and the state.

Toward the end of the nineteenth century, "American abundance was so staggering that the garbage that accumulated daily in cities like New York could support a shadow system of food distribution operated largely by immigrants," Jane Ziegelman writes in *97 Orchard: An Edible History of Five Immigrant Families in One New York Tenement.* "The rag-picker was a key player in this shadow economy, redistributing her daily harvest to peddlers, restaurants, and neighborhood groceries. In her own kitchen, the rag-picker's culinary gleanings formed the basis of a limited but nourishing diet."[1] By the 1880s, this job was typically done by poor and working-class women who immigrated to lower Manhattan from southern Italy. Middle-class New Yorkers—the descendants of earlier generations of immigrants who had settled in Manhattan, on stolen Lenape land—reviled ragpickers, but their work digging through upper-crust trash bins allowed these women to feed their families and communities. Cabbage and onions went into soup, tomatoes were bartered for macaroni, and leftover citrus was cooked into sweet-bright marmellata. The gleaning traditions Italians brought with them from their agricultural hometowns allowed them to make sautés and broth with cicoria, or dandelion greens, harvested each spring from empty lots across the city.[2]

In 1883, the gleaners were considered "the lowest of the low, and yet they seem to be as happy as their neighbors and social associates," as the *New York Times* marvels in an article,[3] unaware of what the women who made up the bulk of this occupation must have known: that there was more food available to them in Manhattan's waste bins than in the wheat fields and olive orchards they had left behind in Italy; that it was greed, not scarcity, that drove hunger in this "land of bread and work."[4] This remains true today: 30 to 40 percent of the US food supply goes to waste annually[5]—unsold, spoiled, or left to rot in landfills because it's blemished or to keep prices high[6]—and even before demands for aid skyrocketed due to the impacts of the COVID-19 pandemic, over 12 percent of NYC residents experienced food insecurity each year.[7]

At the turn of the twentieth century, the Lower East Side was the most densely populated neighborhood in the world, but by the 1970s that population had dwindled. Industrial decline and fiscal crises were followed by planned shrinkage: the intentional withdrawal of city services, from fire departments to libraries, in communities deemed unable or unfit to survive, a decision that was invariably racist and classist in nature.[8] Landlords, left with half-empty high-rises or rents that couldn't be raised, torched buildings for insurance money, leaving a landscape that Malve von Hassell, in her book *The Struggle for Eden: Community Gardens in New York City*, likened to "abandoned and crumbling buildings and vacant lots giv[ing] it the appearance of a blackened slab of Swiss cheese."[9]

Neighborhood residents—many of whom were part of an upswing in Puerto Rican migration to the city in the 1940s and '50s—began clearing abandoned, rubble-strewn lots and turning them into gardens. These gardens were frequently born out of community cooperation: La Plaza Cultural, started by activists from the Latinx-led organization CHARAS, worked with Liz Christy of the group Green Guerillas, who scattered seed bombs and planted willow and linden trees,[10] while Carmen Pabón, a self-proclaimed "social worker without a license"[11] who painted, wrote poetry, and collaborated on street theater about corrupt housing policies,[12] worked with houseless neighbors to found Bello Amanecer Borincano Garden in 1984.[13] While the gardens abounded with fruits, herbs, and vegetables, they also functioned as crucial community gathering spaces: Pabón used Bello Amanecer Borincano as a base from which to distribute food and clothing and housed families who needed a place to stay in the plot's casita;[14] La Plaza Cultural doubles as a performance space and, for a time in the late 1980s, housed a tent city and soup kitchen.[15]

Starting in 1978, New York City's gardens were semiprotected by "Operation Green Thumb," which legally recognized the autonomously built green spaces. However, gardens were considered a temporary use of space, and leases were easily canceled. Miranda J. Martinez, in *Power at the Roots: Gentrification, Community Gardens, and the Puerto Ricans of the Lower East Side*, notes that "the land could be sold for development without consultations with gardeners on site."[16] By the early 1980s, gentrification had begun, driven, in part, by artists moving into the neighborhood, many of whom were of white, middle-class backgrounds. "Art that incorporated urban blight as an aesthetic theme effectively helped to market the Lower East Side as a new bohemia," Martinez writes. "New investment and a new class of residents began to move in." Many of these newcomers were drawn by developers who refurbished old buildings and marketed them as cheap living and studio spaces.[17] By the 1990s, garden land became desirable for housing developments and—particularly under Rudy Giuliani's tenure as mayor—were targeted for removal.[18]

During that same decade, a movement sprouted to defend gardens threatened by development, including Jardín de la Esperanza, originally founded by Alicia Torres in 1978 and run, for the next twenty-two years, by a group of community activists, many of whom lived in the tenant-managed building next door. In its prime, Esperanza overflowed with flowers, vegetables, grapes, and the sound of people gathering in and around the casita that anchored the space, but in 1999 the city approved sale of the land to developer BFC Partners.[19] Donald Capoccia, a principal in the firm, had a reputation for razing gardens and wanted to build an apartment building—80 percent luxury housing, with only 20 percent reserved for working-class residents—on the site. A coalition formed, including members of other gardens, activists from Times Up! and Reclaim the Streets, and squatters who occupied abandoned buildings across the Lower East Side.[20] While some fought for Esperanza in the courts, others took direct action, installing sleeping dragons and other lockdown devices in the garden, including one in the shape of a sunflower.[21] From late 1999 to early 2000, garden defenders kept vigil from the giant canvas-and-mesh coquí, a frog endemic to Puerto Rico and symbolic of the island, perched on Esperanza's fence. In a 1999 article for the *Village Voice* by J.A. Lobbia, Alicia Torres's son Jose Torres said, "There are many myths about the coquí in Puerto Rico, and one is that a monster came stomping through town one night terrorizing people," and the tiny coquí with its big cry was the only animal able to deter it. "A coqui is tiny, but it got rid of the monster," Aresh, a garden defender, continued. "We gardeners are tiny, but we want to save the garden by making a lot of noise."[22]

While many gardens still punctuate the Lower East Side, Jardín de la Esperanza was among those that were ultimately lost. On February 15, 2000—two hours before a temporary restraining order was handed down to halt the destruction of any Green Thumb gardens—bulldozers arrived at Esperanza. After removing locked-down protesters and arresting thirty-one people for resisting arrest, criminal trespass, and obstruction of government process, the bulldozers leveled the rose bushes, arbor, casita, and lovingly tended vegetable plots. The rooster that lived in the garden was safely removed shortly before the destruction began.[23]

On those Sundays in 2006, Food Not Bombs would finish cooking by the early afternoon. We loaded the trays of salad and pots of soup into shopping carts and wheeled the food a mile away to Tompkins Square Park, weaving past many of the gardens I'd heard about around the prepping table and would, years later, read about in greater detail. Vines cascaded over gates, splashes of orange daylilies lined pathways, and, passing the Sixth Street & Avenue B Community Garden, I'd peer up at Eddie Boros's sixty-five-foot toy tower, made of recycled treasures and planks of wood.[24] A block and a half past the garden, we turned our carts left and entered Tompkins, the noisy green heart of Lower East Side counterculture and resistance.

Unlike many soup kitchens and food pantries, Food Not Bombs groups see their meals as a form of direct action against capitalism's waste, government spending on militarization instead of nourishment,[25] and the criminalization of sharing food in public spaces. "It is the Food Not Bombs position that we have a right to give away free food anytime, anywhere, without any permission from the state," write Keith McHenry and C.T. Lawrence Butler in the book *Food Not Bombs*.[26]

McHenry and Butler were part of the first Food Not Bombs collective, founded in Massachusetts in 1981 as an outgrowth of the antinuclear movement. Since then, Food Not Bombs groups have been repeatedly shut down, fined, and detained for sharing food. San Francisco was a frequent site of these interruptions, most notably when fifty-four volunteers were arrested on a single day in 1988 in Golden Gate Park.[27] "After the police have left the area bring out more food but still leave some hidden so if the police come back you will still have more to serve," reads step two of a how-to entitled "If the Police Start Taking Your Food" included in *Food Not Bombs*, while step three assures the reader that "Very rarely do the police come back a third time because they are already feeling very foolish by the second time."[28] Although Manhattan Food Not Bombs has seen its share of police busts—part of a longer history of resistance and repression in Tompkins Square Park—throughout the year or so I volunteered, we were never disrupted.

Young and eager, Sebastian and I did whatever we were asked once we arrived at the park, which sometimes meant laying out zines or handing out bread, and other times ladling hot soup into bowls—I was careful not to spill and shyly mumbled a response when the diners offered up a thank-you. These were often houseless community members who spent their days in Tompkins, chatting and playing chess or music, although everyone who wanted to was invited to eat or volunteer to prepare the meal. This was a pushback against church- or city-based programs that demanded faith or proof of economic hardship in exchange for food and created sharp distinctions between those receiving and giving aid.

After everyone was served and the crowd had dwindled, I filled my own bowl, dipping bread into a lentil soup or ginger-laced curry that had been cooked up with whatever was donated that week. As I ate, I looked out over the park: the tree-lined avenues, the lawn where train hoppers hung out all summer, and the park benches designed, so the rumors went, with armrests placed close together so people couldn't stretch out and take a nap.

In 2019, I took a tour of Tompkins with Bill Weinberg, a writer who works with the Museum of Reclaimed Urban Space. I scribbled notes anytime he mentioned the radical food history of the park and later, by parsing through books and newspaper articles, created a sort of mental map.

A relief garden was planted in Tompkins during the Great Depression. Thousands of children were issued four-by-four plots to plant vegetables, and harvests were shared equally among them.[29] Nearby, soup kitchens were set up at newly formed Catholic Workers' Houses of Hospitality, borne from a Christian anarchist movement centered on voluntary poverty, prefigurative politics, and works of mercy.[30]

"The famous Digger stew, which is made daily in a huge white-enameled pot in a kitchen behind the office, is ladled out—free, of course—to anyone who wants it every afternoon around five o'clock in Tompkins Square Park," reads a *New Yorker* "Talk of the Town" article from 1967 about a faction of the theater-centric anarchist group that made the Lower East Side home in the 1960s. "When Clyde, Susan, Diego, and Richie are asked to explain why they are performing these services for the lower East Side community, each repeats the enigmatic Digger motto: 'Diggers do.'"[31] The Diggers saw sharing free food as a way to teach people about their anticapitalist ideals, and in San Francisco diners had to walk through a giant wooden "Frame of Reference" before they were served.[32]

Formerly a settlement house for recently arrived immigrants, the Christodora at East Ninth Street and Avenue B was home to chapters of the Young Lords and the Black Panthers in the 1960s, and both groups ran free breakfast programs for children. One of these programs, run by the Young Lords on the Lower East Side, fed about twenty-five children each school day. "The reason that the YLP has these free breakfast programs is that many of our children go to school hungry every day," reads an article from the newspaper *Palante* published on July 3, 1970. "In order for us to have a thinking mind we must have a full stomach. Free Breakfast Programs will not change the racist brainwashing education system in this country, but they do deal with the immediate physical needs of our people."[33]

St. Brigid's Church, located a block from the Christodora, was built by Irish immigrants fleeing the Great Hunger of the 1840s and nicknamed "the Famine Church."[34] Over a hundred years later—during what Weinberg calls the Class War period, which stretched from the late 1980s to early 1990s and began with a pitched battle in the park in which unhoused activists and anarchists faced off with the police—students at St. Brigid's School brought food to people occupying Tompkins in tents. Leftovers from the school's lunch program were legally supposed to be thrown away so, as Pastor George Kuhn told Clayton Patterson in an interview, the cafeteria workers would "put the unused food in a marked black garbage bag that they put out as trash" and he would collect and distribute it. Once, Kuhn crossed a police line with other religious leaders to deliver food to activists occupying an abandoned school, and when the police said that they were under orders to not let anyone through, he replied: "I'm following orders too. To give food to the hungry and drink to the thirsty." The ministers crossed the line, hoisted up the food on pulleys, and were arrested.[35]

These days I live across the country, and I last visited ABC No Rio on a Sunday in 2018, a year after the building was bulldozed. Peering through the construction hoarding, I found an empty lot: ailanthus and knotweed sprung up where the tenement's foundation once lay. An orange boom lift pointed upward a few yards from where the stairwell had stood, and I imagined walking up those dimly lit steps into the kitchen where I first learned the value of mutual aid. I imagined picking up a knife and crushing garlic under the flat side so many times that its pungence sunk into my hands and stayed there for days, and listening to the other volunteers tell stories that suggested another world was possible.

I know that spaces created outside of or in resistance to capitalism are often ephemeral. In the case of ABC No Rio, the collective has fundraised millions of dollars to put a new, building-code-approved structure on the property—models show a tall, sleek structure built to maximize space and the possibilities of alternative energy, with vines cascading down the façade[36]—but construction hasn't started yet. In that moment, standing in front of the emptied lot, the world felt a little more tenuous than usual, a feeling underscored by the scent of coffee wafting down the block from a new, three-dollar-a-cup café. But later that same day, I walked through the Lower East Side, by the community gardens and through Tompkins Square Park. Past the dog park and the green lawn, where hipsters had replaced train hoppers, I saw a folding table filled with soup, bread, and salad. The volunteers behind it were busily ladling out bowls, and a banner reading "Food Not Bombs" hung off the front: a reminder that some things, after all, remain.

An earlier version of "Abundance and Other Lessons on the Lower East Side" was published at Blind Field: A Journal of Cultural Inquiry *on June 15, 2020.*

Notes

1   Jane Ziegelman, *97 Orchard: An Edible History of Five Immigrant Families in One New York Tenement* (New York: Harper, 2010), 191.
2   Ziegelman, *97 Orchard*, 188–215.

3   "Found in Garbage-Boxes," *New York Times*, July 15, 1883.

4   Ziegelman, *97 Orchard*, 207–8.

5   "Food Waste FAQS," US Department of Agriculture, accessed August 8, 2021, https://www.usda.gov/foodwaste/faqs.

6   Suzanne Goldenberg, "The US Throws Away as Much as Half Its Food Produce," *Wired*, July 14, 2016, https://www.wired.com/2016/07/us-throws-away-much-half-food-produce/.

7   "Research and Reports," Food Bank for New York City, accessed September 7, 2022, https://www.foodbanknyc.org/research-reports/.

8   Deborah Wallace and Rodrick Wallace, "Benign Neglect and Planned Shrinkage," Verso Books blog, March 25, 2017, https://www.versobooks.com/blogs/3145-benign-neglect-and-planned-shrinkage.

9   Malve von Hassell, *The Struggle for Eden: Community Gardens in New York City* (Westport, CT: Bergin & Garvey, 2002), 53.

10   "History," La Plaza Cultural de Armando Perez Community Garden, accessed August 8, 2021, http://www.opencity.com/laplazacultural/history/.

11   Imani Vieira, "Carmen Pabón, La Madrina De Loisaida," *The People's LES*, May 6, 2020, https://www.peoplesles.org/carmen-pabon-la-madrina-de-loisaida/.

12   Miranda J. Martinez, *Power at the Roots: Gentrification, Community Gardens, and the Puerto Ricans of the Lower East Side* (Lanham, MD: Lexington Books, 2010), 83.

13   Von Hassell, *Struggle for Eden*, 6.

14   Martinez, *Power at the Roots*, 83.

15   Von Hassell, *Struggle for Eden*, 69.

16   Martinez, *Power at the Roots*, 26–27.

17   Martinez, *Power at the Roots*, 16.

18   Sarah Shearman, "In New York City's Lower East Side, Gardening Is a Political Act of Resistance," *Guardian*, August 11, 2015, https://www.theguardian.com/lifeandstyle/2015/aug/11/new-york-lower-east-side-community-gardens.

19   Von Hassell, *Struggle for Eden*, 59–63.

20   Ben Shepherd, "Esperanza, Garden of Hope," TenantNet, accessed August 8, 2021, http://tenant.net/tengroup/Metcounc/Mar00/Esperanza.html.

21   Von Hassell, *Struggle for Eden*, 61.

22   J.A. Lobbia, "The Coqui vs. the Bulldozer," *Village Voice*, November 23, 1999, https://www.villagevoice.com/1999/11/23/the-coqui-vs-the-bulldozer/.

23   Von Hassell, *Struggle for Eden*, 59–62.

24   Dana, "Remembering the Toy Tower," Off the Grid (Village Preservation blog), July 1, 2011, https://www.villagepreservation.org/2011/07/01/remembering-the-toy-tower/.

25   C.T. Lawrence Butler and Keith McHenry, *Food Not Bombs* (Tucson, AZ: See Sharp Press, 2000), 1–5.

26   Lawrence and McHenry, *Food Not Bombs*, 22.

27   Lawrence and McHenry, *Food Not Bombs*, 80–100.

28   Lawrence and McHenry, *Food Not Bombs*, appendix.

29   Sarah Ferguson, "A Brief History of Grassroots Greening in NYC," in *Under the Asphalt: Community Gardens in New York City*, 1999, https://interactivist.net/gardens/h_1.html.

30   Anne Klejment, "From Union Square to Heaven," in *Radical Gotham: Anarchism in New York City from SCHWAB'S Saloon to Occupy Wall Street*, ed. Tom Goyens (Urbana: University of Illinois Press, 2017), 109–11.

31   "Free Store (New York)," *New Yorker*, October 14, 1967, in the Digger Archives, accessed August 8, 2021, https://diggers.org/free_store1.htm.

32   Warren J. Belasco, *Appetite for Change: How the Counterculture Took On the Food Industry* (Ithaca, NY: Cornell University Press, 2007), 17.

33   Darrel Enck-Wanzer, *The Young Lords: A Reader* (New York: New York University Press, 2010), 220.

34   David Scharfenberg, "Coming Back to Fight for the Church of Their Ancestors," *New York Times*, 2006, https://www.nytimes.com/2006/06/18/nyregion/thecity/18chur. html.

35   Clayton Patterson, Joe Flood, and Alan Moore, "An Interview with Father George Kuhn, Former Pastor of St. Brigid's Church," in *Resistance: A Radical Political and Social History of the Lower East Side*, ed. Clayton Patterson (New York: Seven Stories Press, 2007), 119–20.

36   "A New Building," ABC No Rio, accessed August 8, 2021, http://www.abcnorio.org/ newbuilding.php.

Uthando Luvunwa Apha:
A Postcapitalist Love Story

te'sheron courtney

After the plagues, the world ended. With each new vaccine, a new mutation appeared. The survival rate remained high for years, but Jua had been
one of the earliest lands to experience more contagious and dangerous
variants.[1] Around the world, empires crumbled.

"Sthwanda sam" echoed behind my thoughts.[2]

Under the umbrella of the International Organization of Capitalistic
Development and Democracy, wealthier territories had committed to
supporting the distribution of vaccinations to the world's poorest countries. For an entire year, they debated amongst themselves. Thirty-two
countries—of which seventeen had vaccinated more than 70 percent
of their remaining populations, and some had even begun their third
vaccination campaign—debated when and how many residents of the
remaining 163 countries would live. Unlike the plagues of the 2020s, the
BC-3 pandemic would require farther-reaching vaccination campaigns
swiftly.

After a year, *the rift* happened…

"Court."

My life partner's soft words brought me back to consciousness.

"Court, the greenhouse is filled with little humans eager to touch
things." I heard the words but almost instinctively answered, "Huh?"

They tilted their head with a gentle smile as I stood and moved toward
my shoes. "I received an answer from our friends from Litoral," they said.[3]
"They will need to feed twenty-three families while they commute…"

My mind transitioned to the community children that were waiting
for their lesson and lunch. *Did I prune the tomato vines yesterday?*

I spoke directly into their ear as we held an embrace before departing
the room. "Please send the numbers to the monitor in the greenhouse

and ask Ba Pho to send them to the council. The council will discuss at dinner."

Both afternoon lessons moved rather quickly. The first group was filled with youth of confirmation age, followed by the youngens who came to wash and tray harvested fruit and have smoothies immediately after their family lessons.

Five-year-olds are always excited to share what they've learned. As I walked, I thought of a previous conversation where two little ones discussed the rift. "The earth split into pieces," one shouted. The other shot facts right back, saying, "My Umi says the earth stopped working in other places, and so everyone lives in Jua now." Then they both spoke over each other: "Yeah, because of the big big companies and bad medicine." "And everyone can make decisions now." The remainder of their conversation drifted from my thoughts as I arrived at the greenhouse.

In the greenhouse, the ten-to-fourteen-year-olds were all moving around, weaving in and out of various group conversations that sometimes dissolved into one conversation before splitting back off with more personal chats occurring in pockets of two or three. I had been standing in the open doorway, observing quietly, for only a moment when Asahn saw me.

I have known Asahn all of his life. My partner was a member of his family team after his birth and the subsequent passing of his birth-giver. The second oldest child assumed their family's eldership and remained in their family home; the eldest returned with their partners and children. She built an adjacent house on their family land. Her family would receive an elder representation a few years later. Many decisions were made in Asahn's first years, as he was born with a developmental anomaly impacting his muscle development. It was believed Asahn's legs would eventually reach a stage of permanent impairment.

As a teen, Asahn often assisted with meals; I had learned much of his personality when he worked in tandem with other youth on the sanitation team and attended council meetings with his older sibling, the elder of their family. He was a well-informed member of the community, solemn but present in council meetings. He was vocal in his advisement regarding his family's council votes.

His confirmation was the month before. He had decided that he wanted to be addressed as Asahn Leafgreen and be observed as a *boy*. Today was the first time he'd been at harvest since that time. I expected his people had taken him to the surrounding communities to share the announcements and receive blessings. His confirmation was the second time Asahn received blessings from the communities. While he was still young, he was part of the decision to pursue additional medical care that could ensure his ability to walk. At age five, representatives from many communities, many of them using various assistance to support their walking, came to offer their blessings before he began the regimen.

Asahn looked at me for a moment, maybe discerning my energy, and then spoke loudly and with a new depth in his voice. In his home vernacular, he called to the group with our community call and response, our group greeting. Each of them alerted, turned, and without hesitation responded; an array of mother tongues echoed through the farmhouse.

We renovated the edifice upon our arrival to Zama Futhi, building one of the first greenhouses of its kind in the rifted land. Now there were forty-seven greenhouses and four stretches of farmland in Futhi.

I smiled and gave personal greetings to each youth as I walked through the maze of plant life. Often the learners would call me Doc, echoing what they'd heard in council meetings, although the title held little meaning now.

By the end of the second lesson, enough squash was harvested for roughly three days further. For lunch, the little ones prepared smoothies with greens and berries. The teens made tacos, using the freshly picked tomatoes for a zesty salsa.

The maize harvested over the previous weeks had finally yielded corn tortillas, prepared by Ba and Bub Pho. Like me, they were immigrants before the plagues, and when the rift happened, they remained and dedicated themselves to transformation. Ba Pho had been a force on the committees for redistribution and was the most elder representative on our community council. With their leadership, we ensured more than forty-five communities in our region had running-water taps. As more settlements organized the concurrent integration of running water in all homes and set up irrigation systems, Ba Pho and I traveled to any communities that requested assistance.

During our travels, we'd learned a great deal about each other. We shared a language that was not a traditional vernacular from the Jua homelands. It was her first language and one I had not spoken significantly in adulthood, but our friendship had evolved bound by the cultural understanding a shared language brings. We also both had transitioned when it was still culturally taboo, and Ba many years before me.

Ba, Bub, and I were each from across the western ocean. We'd all relocated for various reasons, at different times, and settled among the community, adopting the Indigenous cultures and traditions. Ba came from farming people and was academically achieved as an engineer. Upon relocation, she'd worked with redevelopment organizations to install mechanisms for harvesting water during droughts. She often said it had been her first life, but their industrious energy never left them.

Many of the communities we visited did not need assistance; instead, they wanted to share how their dreams of liberation manifested and talk of the barriers the new world presented to the more capitalistic values still to be unlearned. And we were just the pair for such reckoning. Our journeys had started nearly twenty-five years past.

Over seven hundred communities—rarely ever larger than 1,500 families—speckled the region known as Jua. We had passed the development baton on to younger advisors almost a decade before the people of Litoral were uprooted.

At the first wave of plagues, many municipalities did not have access to clean drinking water. Many had for years walked kilometers in pursuit of water, a day's worth carried on a child's, sometimes an elder's, head. Many of these areas suffered significant losses before the rift, caused by the viruses and the ongoing impacts from the old governments' lack of investment in human needs.

The five-year-olds, though missing some context, simplified the history quite accurately. The mass vaccine production and dissemination in wealthier nations intensified other natural disasters caused by climate instability. Lands became barren, people died, governments *convened*, and people revolted. Even in Jua, the governments fell, and people grew hungrier. Eventually, local scientists would trigger a replication of the prehistoric tectonic movement to conserve the remaining fertile soil.

Sitting at my desk in the rear of the greenhouse, I recalled the files my partner had sent earlier. I transferred the spreadsheet to a projected view: *Physical map of the northern zone 53B*. As the computer readied the hologram, I reached for my glasses. Not immediately finding them, I stood, and my eyes surveyed the east wing of the greenhouse, where the little ones had congregated to pour and drink their smoothies earlier.

Atop a tub of microgreens, I could see the gold rim of my glasses on a table near the tomatoes and cucumbers. I walked toward the sun's refraction in the lenses. Just as I reached the table, my device began to vibrate and ring. I cautiously raised my wrist for the notification to project; I didn't want to risk motioning too swiftly and answering a call I had no desire to take. Many things had changed over the many moon cycles of our lives without empire, but my lack of interest in phone calls had not been one of them.

It had taken years for technical resources to reach us in Jua, but technological advancements occurred regularly now. Futhi did not produce any software or hardware or mine raw materials. Still, the collective of our region was recognized numerous times for medical technology. One of the principal goals of modern medicine was to produce human-centered advancement in collaboration with traditional healing practices. Even after twenty-five Julian years, the plagues' biological effects were more disastrous than we had ever imagined.

Children and teenagers had been the most likely to survive the plagues; they were also the most likely to live with disabilities. Most of us identified as disabled on the universal census of 2060, the first of its kind. Supporting the disabled was always central to the agenda for the Community on Living and was prioritized for research funding. Any and all decisions, like that of Asahn's surgery, were taken with great care.

The ringing grew louder.

Managing my attention span had taken a toll after years of manic-driven academic and strategy labor. I took pleasure in working with the communities rifted. Still, this work of growing, harvesting, and cooking is the one that I'd imagined for myself. Rest was a founding principle of the Collective Collaboration of New Equitable Lands. There were no disappointments when I departed from Senior Advisory to teach, notably as Ba Pho had stepped down several years prior.

My arm grew heavy as my wrist dangled, and the blaring noise from my antique wrist device reverberated. I looked at the notification, which, from the sound pattern that reregistered in my ears, was not a phone call. A series of communiques came through: there was an ongoing conversation occurring in a digital town hall forum, and the transcript was reaching me.

I returned to my desk and sat. Clicking the implant embedded behind my left ear, I joined the forum. I listened in, simultaneously looking at the mountainous terrain the Litoral families would need to travel through. Their community had been established along the eastern coastline a short four years prior. The ceremonial ratification of their charter was one of my final acts as a Collective Senior Advisor.

At that time, there had not been disastrous storms in nearly ten years. But this year, almost fifteen years since the last one, there had been an earthquake in the ocean twenty kilometers off the southernmost coast and subsequently a series of disastrous tsunamis. Most families had relocated inland before the disaster. No one had expected three fishing communities to be wiped out, and redevelopment didn't seem viable from erosion predictions.

Many relocated families stayed inland and made new homes among other communities, but a subset of families voiced restlessness. They wanted to return to their way of life as fisherfolk. Many community councils met individually to hear their petition. Through the forum, we came together collectively; the families sought resettlement, and it was decided they would travel north toward the rift and reestablish there with land for expansion. This decision came after multiple votes and drone explorations of the area.

In just seven ukushona kwelanga, the twenty-three families would begin their voyage.[4] They would travel by ship to Zone 53 to survey the coastline; from there, they would caravan to the precinct identified to establish off the coast. The previous nation-state borders identified the zones, but they were only used for geographical distinction. Most learning circles had only taught the young of the natural boundaries for some twenty years. I'd dusted off some geography texts to study the historical fishing patterns when consulted about the petition.

Once they arrived, fisherfolk would need to stay at the coast, studying the tide, the types of fish, and their patterns. It would be essential to ensure the fish were safe and edible by observing other wildlife on the land. In the interim, the families would need food. With successful fishing, there would also be crops to plant and irrigation systems to establish.

As a harvesting community, Futhi would provide one-eighth of gathers for the travelers, two farmers, seeds of at least thirty crops, and any food-related resources to support them. The communique shared from Senior Advisors included the region's geographical specs; the list of families, with ages and medical and dietary history; and a report that I'd consulted on, which analyzed the drone-photographed vegetation in the area. Futhi's council would need to discuss which items and farmers to send with these families at the twilight meal.

Supper.

The sun had shifted over to the west side of the greenhouse. The kitchen team would already be busy. I gathered my things and turned the digital public participatory media forum off—the only information I had understood from my *listening* was many folks still had opinions about establishing near the rift. However, the decision was final.

As my first visit to Kliptown Youth Program in 2017 had taught me, washing our hands is a practice of community and humility.[5] Today, no different, six youth stood along the structure; ba pethe indishi yo geza izandla[6]—their warm smiles invigorated the cooling water one partner poured over my hands. The tradition preceded every meal as we still passed our ramequins to dish, despite the plagues.

Our community council consisted of a representative from every family that had self-selected to participate. Families could alternate representatives each year or abstain altogether. As Futhi had been one of the earliest established, many families had borne new generations, increasing our council circle. Our community included 420 families. The council had 427 members, with four families abstaining.

The large dining tables held about two hundred but did not fill the room. A rectangle pattern of tables sat in the center of the room, with smaller tables speckling the outlying area. Bold, vibrant laughter rumbled through the Hall of Healing People.

It would take at least thirty minutes for everyone to receive a plate, and when I arrived, some folks had eaten, and a few had left. The second kitchen team finished dishing and found their seats as Ba Pho began to speak. Ba's voice came through the auditory receptor device into my implant, and she was projected to the entire hall. But their voice also echoed as they stood to the far right of me. They were easily heard, even when far yonder in their cornfields. Ba Pho was almost mystical at over two and a half meters tall, with body distributed across that height. Even when I had met them as a leader at KYP before my relocation, her brilliance had lingered.[7]

"Comrades, you've all received the briefing, and the most up-to-date stored harvest is coming to you all now." Pho clicked the handle of her glasses to transmit and adjusted the hearing device in their ear. I watched

Ba Pho as everyone scrolled through the document they'd received to their optical receptor.

Immediately the room echoed with a mesh of vernaculars. Asahn's sibling-guardian spoke first in their mother tongue. "Today's collective forum revealed much more to consider, Pho." The speech translator flooded.

Everyone knew that sending a community in such proximity to the rift could be dangerous, and I could tell today's forum had only heightened concerns.

Ba's eyes caught mine, and I could see they were going to give a proclamation. Pho was my oldest comrade; we'd been together since the time before the first virus and long before the rift. We shared a sacred belief that had become Futhi's slogan of sorts; our call and response and location markers were pseudonyms.

"Comrades, I know many of you are concerned about the safety of these families. I ask you all to recall the time before the rift. People believed intrinsically in individualism, and capitalism was driven by controlling the innovation potential of others. We were not people; we were production capital. After the rift, we were allowed to relearn the ways we exist. We leaned into our innate need for others to rebuild. At which time, we honored the skills of each human and animal alike. Our comrades from Litoral desire a life where they can fish, which is the only way they will holistically survive. Fisherfolk are the bridge between the earth and the ocean."

Community members sighed and nodded. Pho continued, and their words surprised me. "I will travel with the voyage, and I implore our communities to think of generations to come. They will know we did not dictate the means of production of our fellow folk." I turned my body toward Pho's voice. They heard my disbelief and looked toward me, now holding my partner's leg. In their mother tongue, they called to the hall, "Community grows where love is grown," and the hall roared in sound. I joined the chorus: "Love grows here, and we grow here in community."

Litoral North, the flagship of the Northern Rift Region, was ratified into the Collective twenty-three moon cycles later. Pho represented the ancestors at this, my final ceremony, the first without them.

The title of this piece, "Uthando Luvunwa Apha," means, "Love Grows Here." From the isiXhosa language, it literally translates to "love is harvested here."

Notes

1   *Jua* (isiXhosa) has several translations in various languages, including "the sun."
2   "Sthwanda sam" (isiZulu) translates to "My love."
3   *Litoral* (Portuguese) means "coastline, seaside, shore, coastal."
4   *Ukushona kwelanga* (isiZulu) means "sunset."
5   Kliptown Youth Program is a safe space for children to learn, have fun, work together, and prepare themselves to be successful. The organization is based in Kliptown, Soweto, South Africa. KYP offers programs that support youth to lift themselves out of poverty. KYP was founded in May 2017 by young people from Kliptown.
6   From isiZulu, this translates as, "They are holding the bowl—a bowl that is a washbasin."
7   *KYP* stands for Kliptown Youth Program.

Are You a Kindergarden Abolitionist? A List of What's Possible in the Next Economy

sumi dutta

> The first rule of ecological restoration is the restoration of our own labor. Human labor is the precious natural resource, concentrated, controlled and exploited, that has been wielded like a chainsaw against the rest of the natural world. Because of this, we must take it back from the chains of the market and restore it to the web of life.
> —Movement Generation[1]

Many of us wake up and find ourselves working j-o-b-s that are hardly the most delicious use of our labor. I'm really not feeling that for us. If you know deep down inside that your hands are made for crafting mutual aid potions, harvesting seeds for the neighborhood seed bank, and fixing lemon balm tea before teaching a class on how to give an apology—and yet you're spending most of your days laboring outside your purpose—this list is for you.

This may be an unpopular opinion amongst my revolutionary kin, but I love to work. I say this while uncomfortably aware of the ways my high-caste South Asian and American identity has consumed the lie that my people can earn our belonging in this country through hard work. I write this with the purpose of fighting for a solidarity economy and the annihilation of caste. I love work because I believe our lives and our labor are incredibly precious, which is why I loathe the way we're forced to live inside a capitalist, extractive economy. For me, loving to work doesn't look like eight-plus-hour days, depleting our life force for survival or "success." Work is in dynamic balance with everything else—being a politicized community member, tending to our friendships and chosen families, cooking good food and cleaning up after. Our basic needs are met, no matter how much or how little we work. It may sound unfathomable, but as the many unstoppable consequences of climate apocalypse come for us as a species, I know this next economy is already on the way.

Abolition of capitalism and the prison industrial complex invites us to reimagine roles, structures, and care work at the edges of what the ruling class believes is possible. So, what does that actually look like and where do we start? How do we initiate a million small experiments that satisfy our (broken) hearts? Experiments that offer radical community medicine, beyond the band-aid solutions of food banks and the harm of a fatphobic, anti-Black medical industry?

This list is about not being afraid to get specific about what we do in the next economy, so that we can tap into a deeper, soul-shifting feeling of what's possible. It's full of impermanent, interdependent, life-giving labors that move us toward the nourishing, imperfect antidotes we really care about. Their impact doesn't depend on their success—failing at any of the roles on this list only increases how generative they are. There is no failing in the work of radical, life-affirming world building—just more practice and useful lessons. These ideations activate that place in us that is ready to claim our right to build community-based economies, beyond the state.

1. *The Flamingo First Aid Herbal Gang.* We dress up in fashion that pushes our imaginations and walk the streets of our invisible sidewalk neighborhood. We coordinate variations of the same outfit, wearing clothes dyed with black walnut hulls, pecan husks, turmeric, and avocado peels. We make Pinterest boards of our favorite herbs for inspo. We are femme androgynous, wearing thrifted ball gowns and athleisure suits. We are compelling neighbors because we are coordinated wilderness. We take daily walks for fifteen to twenty minutes in the early morning. We make the neighborhood yours by being flamingos that live there; you belong because we belong there with you. First, folks make comments about our fashion. Next, they ask what we are about. We tell them we are community healers and to reach out—we make home visits if needed. We carry first-aid herbal bags in case there is a need in the moment and our neighbors start to call on us.

2. *The Medicinal Florist.* Make bouquets from neighborhood flowers and medicinal weeds. Drop them off at every doorstep on the block with the names of the herbs and their healing properties.

On the bouquet tag, invite folks to a neighborhood plant walk at nine a.m. on Saturday. Meet in front of the Walgreens to learn about the plants nearby. Record and caption the walk to share with folks at home.

3. *The Kindergarden Abolitionist.* Use plants to practice consent with kids. Show them a patch of dandelion plants or a fig tree in the neighborhood. Invite them to ask the plant for permission before they harvest the fruit or leaves. We become what we practice. Remind them that the plant experiences everything that happens in the neighborhood. Ask them what they feel the plant would say about how to best take care of each other.

4. *The Herbal Life Coach.* Have a conversation with a person who is struggling to find their purpose and gift. Learn their birth date, time, and location and pull up their birth chart on chaninicholas.com. Based on what you read, design a vision board collage or "first-aid kit" that reflects their gifts and potential tools for their unique journey, as you see it. Ask them to take pictures of the plants in their yard: sometimes the medicine we need is right at home. Read about the flower essences and healing properties of the plants that live near them. Include plants as guardians of their vision, and perhaps even guide them through a process of doing this on their own.

5. *The Highway Herbalists.* Since many medicinal herbs grow alongside railroad tracks and highways, the places where the earth has been disturbed for development, these edges are also where the healing can happen for the land and us. The Highway Herbalists remind us that all land is sacred: not just pretty pastures and rolling green hills, but every cemented surface we live on is a breathing one, no matter what we throw on top of it. They practice bodywork on community members in a patch of land off the highway where you can hear the traffic commotion while hands heal you. They practice tai chi, meditation, and qi gong in a grocery-store parking lot. They repair the disconnect of our species versus the land.

6. *The Conflict Transformation Cookbook.* We know time doesn't heal all wounds, but food just might help us metabolize them. Conflict isn't bad news—it helps us build trust and deepen relationships, just like sharing a meal can. In the next economy, we're going to need to build skills for being in principled struggle. Food has a

role to play because it helps conjure a smell-good, feel-good, taste-good memory that stretches our hearts toward community care. Transforming conflict and taking accountability is community care. *The Conflict Transformation Cookbook* blends the wisdom of medicinal herbs, flowers, and the meals that shape us (Ranga ma's aloo and luchi, Mom's begun bhaja, partner's oatmeal-pear pancakes) to attend to the pain points, political disagreements, and hurt feelings that arise when learning how to exist well together. *The Conflict Transformation Cookbook* invites you to open your heart by cooking *and* practicing direct communication. Whip up wild-rose-petal chocolate sauce when you need an ally for communicating boundaries. Make a simple, hearty daal and rice with roasted vegetables when you need to identify your core values. Don't be afraid of food as a metaphor.

7.   *The Free Herbal Grocery.* Medicine that grows from the ground can be free. The Free Herbal Grocery is a community apothecary with donated, wildcrafted, and locally grown plant and allopathic medicine. It's a worker co-op with weekly open hours. Twinkly string lights drape across the rows of dried plant material in ball jars and tinctures in large amber bottles. The grocery is there for folks when the hospital-prescribed medication is too costly but no treatment is not an option. It's solidarity with a community that's reeling from pandemics and other climate disasters, who are choosing to turn toward land-based healing. The grocery distributes first-aid kits for the direct action and suggests herbs for apocalypse-induced insomnia. It makes its home in a small, community-built structure with crowdsourced funds. It shows us that abundance doesn't require much space when one jar of lavender buds ensures the whole block sleeps better.

This essay was inspired by Emergent Strategy, *by adrienne maree brown;* Fumbling Towards Repair: A Workbook for Community Accountability Facilitators, *by Mariame Kaba and Shira Hassan; Movement Generation's Resilience-Based Organizing principles; and my BIPOC herbalism and multiracial organizing community in Durham, North Carolina.*

Note

1   "Resilience-Based Organizing," Movement Generation Justice & Ecology Project, 2013, accessed September 7, 2022, https://movementgeneration.org/resources/key-concepts/resiliencebasedorganizing/.

Seeds Planted by Nana Tota

Nelda Ruiz

I am five years old, lying on the creaky wooden bed of my Nana Tota's house in El Ranchito, Hermosillo, in Sonora, Mexico. The air still feels fresh, but soon the heat will radiate off the black asphalt rivers and concrete sidewalks outside, an entirely different world than her pueblo of Huásabas. We'll stay cool inside, because Tota has dirt floors that she wets down and sweeps a few times a day. Already I can smell burning mesquite from the cast-iron stove. The smell calls me, and I crawl from bed and go to watch her studiously. I already feel immersed in magic as I walk outside. It seems I'm in a kaleidoscope, because rays of sun hit the broken glass bottles anchored with concrete at the top of the wall that serves as her security system. Her hands are the color of mazapan, with wrinkles as deep as the canyons of Sonora. She gathers more wood, then strategically places each one into the fire like a puzzle. She is preparing for the day's cooking—olla de frijoles, chile colorado, y tortillas sobaqueras— before it gets too hot.

As the fire burns, Nana Tota visits her seedlings: many medicinal plants that have so comfortably found a home in cozy metal coffee tins of various sizes, thanks to her loving and stewarding hands, each one placed with such intention it's evident how healthy and happy they are. My Nana Tota is my great-grandmother, mother of my grandmother Barbarita, and grandmother of Yolanda, my ama. The silver threads on Tota's head sway with the soft breeze. I look up to her and she seems as tall and ancient as a saguaro.

As the fire snaps and cracks, Tota tells me stories about what foods she is preparing and what each plant is used for. "Cilantro," she says, "es para darle vida a la comida y chiltepin." She continues, "Es para darnos vida a nosotros!" Everything is connected, Tota says. What we grow nourishes the Earth and our bodies; we cook what we grow. We treat the plantitas with respect, as we would our family members, because they are also our relatives. My little self absorbs precious abuelita knowledge like a dry sponge in water, her stories planting seeds in my growing soul. These moments in Nana Tota's outdoor kitchen build the foundation for my life: the way we care for the Earth is the way we care for others, and it's a reciprocal relationship. The Earth nourishes us, we nourish the plants, and the plants nourish us. What we eat is who we are—our maíz, our chile, our beans, our calabaza.

For me, continuing to practice traditional ways of growing, cooking, and eating is a way of liberation, a way to counter the systems that keep us oppressed and distant from the land, from that reciprocal relationship. As migrant people heading to el norte, it is easy to lose sight of our roots as the oil of capitalism seeps into our remaining familial units and poisons us. The oil that demands we work multiple jobs to cover our basic necessities (and sometimes still fall short). The oil that makes us work ten-plus-hour days so we're too tired to cook and instead grab a ninety-nine-cent fried-chicken sandwich with papitas. Who has time to make the elaborate enchiladas de chile colorado that would connect us to our home, our ancestors, and the spirit? It's the quick drive-through sandwich or the five-dollar pizza or the Hot Cheetos. Each bite we take slowly erases who we are. And leaves us hungry. That oil fuels us for the next shift or the next migration but doesn't feed our soul.

It has been nearly thirty years since I stood barefoot on the cool, damp earth of my Nana Tota's outdoor kitchen in El Ranchito. She became an ancestor in the mid-1990s, but my memories of her teachings continue to inform my being and practice every day. For so many of us who have been removed from traditional familial practices and land—either by force or by necessity—and now live in places where these practices are undervalued, how do we reconnect to what we've lost?

Poema del frijol
Little spotted being,
Nourishing you are, thank you,
a staple of us.

I am now here in el norte, establishing my root system in what seems like caliche-saturated soil and anchoring myself even if I have to force it, in a place that so desperately tries to make us forget we even have roots at all. So, when those available moments allow me to use my hands to go through each bean one by one, removing rocks and remembering my childhood as I clean, soaking them in special herbs to prepare for cooking, this is the closest practice I have to liberation—that ancestral knowledge, radiating from our ancestral DNA, expanding in our bodies like the spread of pollen in springtime, ensuring we don't forget who we are; our beans hold our stories and we hold theirs.

Today, I am in one of the community backyard gardens that I helped install with Regeneración, a grassroots organizing crew based in the south side of Tucson dedicated to connecting neighbors with the resources they may need to create safe, healthy, and regenerative communities rooted in traditional and ancestral knowledge. Bees are buzzing, drunk with bright yellow pollen saturating their little bodies, and my sweat is dripping slow like honey while I amend a raised bed, prepping it for planting again. I am about to do a skill-sharing workshop with a group of young people from the hood. They're really excited to plant herbs today, but I'm also going to talk about frijoles and how we cook them, how knowledge that we often overlook is one of the richest things we hold. These days, I find myself working like a little ant, carrying fifty times my body weight, spreading my Nana Tota's stories like seeds, flowers, and tending roots. The work I do today is about continuing the teachings Nana Tota planted in me when I was a child. I help youth reconnect to their culture, their beauty, and their ancestors through food, using gardens as a tool for liberation, creating conversations that lead them to think about the intersections of food justice, migrant rights, community safety, and health. Like my Nana Tota, whose hands so confidently and intentionally nurtured her plants (and me), I find myself using the same intention and care to tend my community and create regenerative spaces.

What seeds do you carry with you?

Acknowledgments

It feels funny to offer my own acknowledgments for such a wildly collective project, but there are a few people I need to thank. Much of my initial thinking around food in protest movements and mutual aid came out of conversations with my friend Cheshire Li, whose words appear in the preceding pages, and were inspired by the work of longtime movement cook Mike "Grumble" Bowersox. Thank you to everyone who let me interview you for the original Nourishing Resistance series and to Lela Scott MacNeil, who made space for the series on her site, *Bone + All*. Cindy Barukh Milstein encouraged me to pitch this anthology to PM Press and provided so much support along the way, and Steven Stothard was an incredibly supportive editor. Too many friends to name offered moral and sounding-board support, but I would be remiss not to mention Eshani Surya, Margaret Killjoy, and my BCC Tucson crew (you know who you are!). Thanks to Tyler Espinoza, Goose the cat, my parents, and other family members who have cheered me on as a writer and editor. And a special thanks to anyone who connected me with a contributor or helped in a myriad of other ways: your support means everything.

Above all, thanks to the contributors, who bore with me when I made every first-time editor mistake in the proverbial book and who brought so much to this project. And to you, the reader, for bringing your own creativity, knowledge, and wisdom to these pages.

About the Authors

Wren Awry is a writer, editor, and archivist whose work ranges from researching and writing about the role of food in labor strikes, mutual aid projects, and revolt to helping with community dinners at their local, collectively run social center. They've written about food for publications including *The Rumpus*, *Entropy*, and *Blind Field: A Journal of Cultural Inquiry* and have facilitated various culinary writing classes, including garden poetry for first graders and a community workshop on queer food writing. Most recently, they have been digging through radical, labor, and zine archives to find materials related to food and cooking and are learning to build archives on their own and in collaboration with others.

Alessandra Bergamin is an Australian freelance journalist based in Los Angeles. Her work focuses on environmental justice, gender, and labor and has been published in *The Baffler*, *Harper's*, the *Washington Post*, the *New Yorker*, and *DAME*. She is an IJNR Environmental Justice Reporting Award grantee and a UC Berkeley Food and Farming fellow.

Mike Costello developed an appreciation for the land at an early age, while growing up on a farm in Kanawha County, West Virginia. He also found a home in the kitchen, learning to string pole beans and bake traditional desserts from his grandmother, "Momaw" Betty Williams. After working in West Virginia restaurant kitchens and encountering a then-pervasive mentality that "quality" ingredients must be shipped to Appalachia from far away, he was intrigued by the implications of food narratives for people- and place-based cultures. Mike enrolled in journalism school at West Virginia University and began telling stories about food, heritage, and place. Mike is a chef, freelance writer, media producer, and cohost of *The Pickle Shelf Radio Hour*. He serves on the board of directors for the Appalachian Food Summit and runs Lost Creek Farm with Amy Dawson.

te'sheron courtney is a disruptor. Texas-born. Howard-groomed, and continent-chillin'. Black, queer, plant-based, Pan Africanist, and student of radicalism. Court is a social entrepreneur, equity strategist, and researcher with a deep familial culinary background. Their work often uses cuisine and curated food experiences to bring conversations about the feminization of hunger and other social inequalities that impact Black, women, and queer folks, particularly in the global south, to the table. In all their work, Court (re)builds equity-driven systems that prioritize the emancipation of all Black and other actively marginalized communities.

Luz Cruz is a queer, Afro-Latinx, transgender writer and a food justice organizer. Their work focuses on sustainability and climate change through a racial and gender justice lens.

Lindsey Danis (www.lindseydanis.com) is a queer writer of fiction and essays whose writing has appeared in *Condé Nast Traveler*, *AFAR*, *Fodor's*, and *Longreads*. Lindsey's work centers LGBTQ voices, with a focus on honoring LGBTQ history, celebrating queer joy, and expanding the types of queer stories that get told. Lindsey's essays have received a notable mention in *The Best American Travel Writing* and are forthcoming in several anthologies, including *The Best New True Crime Stories* and *Riding Fences: Essays on Being LGBTQ+ in Rural Areas*. When not writing, Lindsey is often found hiking or kayaking near her Hudson Valley home.

Laurence Desmarais is an organizer and academic whose work focuses on Indigenous solidarity, police abolition, and art. A descendant of French settlers, she lives in Montreal, Canada, on unceded Kanien'kehà:ka and Anishinabe lands.

sumi dutta (she/her) writes queer love letters to plants in her neighborhood, takes daily walks, and practices abolition like it could happen tomorrow. She lives on Occaneechi, Eno, and Shakori Indigenous land and land stewarded by formerly enslaved Black folks, also known as Durham, North Carolina. She is the child of two Bengali immigrants who moved from Calcutta to Durham in the late 1970s, and she is committed to annihilating caste in her family line.

Eating in Public was founded in 2003 in Hawai'i by **Gaye Chan** and **Nandita Sharma**. Chan is a conceptual artist who engages in solo and collaborative activities that take place on the web, in publications, on the streets, and in galleries (gayechan.com). Sharma is an activist scholar whose research is shaped by the social movements she is active in, including No Borders movements and those struggling for the planetary commons (nanditasharma.net). Eating in Public can be found at nomoola.com.

Alyshia Gálvez is a professor of Latin American and Latino studies at Lehman College and of anthropology at the Graduate Center, both of the City University of New York. Her teaching and research are at the intersection of food, health, and migration. She strives to be a reliable accomplice to BIPOC and projects for rights and sovereignty, with particular emphasis on the rights to mobility and food sovereignty.

Shayontoni Rhea Ghosh (she/her) is a writer, theater-maker, facilitator, and magician inspired by the ocean, feminist spirituality, monotonous soundscapes, and *The Book of Changes*.

Paridhi Gupta has a PhD in gender studies from Jawaharlal Nehru University, India. Her work has revolved around the cultural manifestations of feminist social movements in the country. In addition to resistance studies, she also works on public art, digital humanities, and urban studies. Aside from research, she is currently aiming to build peer-support networks for academics from the field of social science and humanities.

Madeline Lane-McKinley is the author of *Comedy Against Work: Utopian Longing in Dystopian Times* (Common Notions, 2022) and an editor for *Blind Field: A Journal of Cultural Inquiry.*

Lausan is a volunteer collective of writers, translators, artists, and organizers whose members are dispersed around the world. Through our writing, translating, and organizing, we build transnational left solidarity and struggle for ways of life beyond the dictates of capital and the state by holding multiple imperialisms to account. We believe a radical imagination of Hong Kong—and global—futures must center grassroots transnational solidarity based on class struggle, migrant justice, antiracism, and feminism.

Cheshire Li is a nonbinary and first-gen Chinese-American photographer, filmmaker, community organizer, and creative. They currently reside on stolen Arapaho, Cheyenne, Núu-agha-tʉvʉ-pʉ (Ute), and Očhéthi Šakówiŋ lands in Denver, Colorado. When they aren't supporting grassroots disaster-relief kitchens in storm season, Cheshire owns and operates their independent pedicab company. They also work as a freelance photographer; in the camera, grip, and electric departments in the film industry; and as the Ambassador Program manager for VIDA women's mountain bike clinics. Cheshire spends their spare time on their mountain bike, riding throughout the high alpine mountains of Colorado and western US; in the winters, you can find them snowboarding and learning to tour the backcountry on a splitboard. Their goal as a queer BIPOC cyclist and adventurer is to elevate and center Indigenous, Black, and brown voices in the outdoors and in film—"because we deserve to tell our own stories in the ways they deserve to be told."

mayam (they/them/theirs) is a Black, trans, queer farmer originally from Catawba Territory (Charlotte, North Carolina) and is currently living on occupied Tiwa Territory (Albuquerque, New Mexico). Farming has been in their family for many generations, and they feel proud to continue the legacy of stewarding the land and being in relationship with the elements. As a member of Seeding Sovereignty, mayam is pursuing their dreams of managing their own farm, as land steward of Ancestral Acres Farm and Garden. Ancestral Acres Farm and Garden is dedicated to growing food for and with the queer and trans community in so-called Albuquerque, New Mexico, as well as distributing food to community members and mutual aid projects, saving seeds, and building healthy soil as a way of paying homage to those who've come before us. As a farmer, mayam recognizes the importance of healthy relationships with land, water, and life. Without our soil, without our water and living ecologies, we would have a hard time living as a people. Furthering the endeavor of growing food, mayam is dedicating their life and practice as a farmer to growing seeds to share with the community, providing transformative spaces for people of the global majority to fellowship, and tending to healthy soils for all to thrive.

Cindy Barukh Milstein, a diasporic queer Jewish anarchist, is the author of *Anarchism and Its Aspirations* and *Try Anarchism for Life* and the editor of anthologies such as *Rebellious Mourning: The Collective Work of Grief*, *Deciding for Ourselves: The Promise of Direct Democracy*, and *There Is Nothing So Whole as a Broken Heart: Mending the World as Jewish Anarchists*. Long engaged in anarchistic organizing and social movements, Milstein is passionate about shaping and sharing magical do-it-ourselves spaces with others, such as, most recently, the Institute for Advanced Troublemaking's Anarchist Summer School and the Montreal Anarchist Bookfair; being a doula for books and mourning; and embodying as much solidarity, collective care, and love as possible. You can find them on Instagram @cindymilstein or via their blog at cbmilstein.wordpress.com.

Nelda Liliana Ruiz Calles is a fronteriza community organizer, cultural worker, and folklorist from the Sonoran borderlands. As a Barrio Campesina (farmer) with Regeneración, she supports young people through popular education in reconnecting to the Earth through traditional ways of knowing and respect. Nelda has been organizing for over eleven years, connecting communities with the resources they may need in order to create safe, healthy, and regenerative communities in the south side of Tucson, Arizona. Nelda is a 2019 National Association of Latino Arts & Cultures (NALAC) Leadership Institute fellow (NLI), a 2019 Adelita Del Año awardee presented by Las Adelitas AZ, and a 2017 Mujer En La Lucha awardee presented by the Arizona Cesar E. Chavez Holiday Coalition.

Katie Tastrom (she/her) is a disabled sex worker and writer and organizer. She is currently working on a book about abolition and disability justice. She lives in upstate New York, and you can find out more by going to her website at katietastrom.com, but it probably needs updating. She's easy to find if you need her.

Virginia Tognola is a journalist, a militant in the Movimiento Popular Nuestramérica, and an independent writer focused on politics, culture, and human and environmental rights.

Virgie Tovar is an author, an activist, and one of the nation's leading experts and lecturers on weight-based discrimination and body image. She holds a master's degree in sexuality studies with a focus on the intersections of body size, race, and gender. She is a contributor for *Forbes*, where she covers the plus-size market and how to end weight discrimination at work. She is the founder of Babecamp, a self-guided online course designed to help people break up with diet culture. She started the hashtag campaign #LoseHateNotWeight and in 2018 gave a TedX Talk on the origins of the campaign. Tovar edited the anthology *Hot & Heavy: Fierce Fat Girls on Life, Love and Fashion* (Seal Press, 2012), and she's the author of *You Have the Right to Remain Fat* (Feminist Press, 2018) and *The Self-Love Revolution: Radical Body Positivity for Girls of Color* (New Harbinger Publications, 2020). Her podcast, *Rebel Eaters Club*, is New York–based Transmitter Media's first original production. In 2018, she was named one of the fifty most influential feminists by *Bitch Magazine*. She has received two San Francisco Arts Commission Individual Artist Commissions as well as Yale's Poynter Fellowship in Journalism. She lives in San Francisco.

Nico Wisler is a Philadelphia-based middle school teacher and audio storyteller. By day, they are constantly honing their storytelling chops by teaching sixth grade. They are the host of Heritage Radio Network's *Queer the Table*, a podcast about LGBTQ+ identity and food. They have also produced for WHYY's *The Pulse*, PRI's *The World*, and the *Food in Two Worlds* podcast.

ABOUT PM PRESS

PM Press is an independent, radical publisher of books and media to educate, entertain, and inspire. Founded in 2007 by a small group of people with decades of publishing, media, and organizing experience, PM Press amplifies the voices of radical authors, artists, and activists. Our aim is to deliver bold political ideas and vital stories to all walks of life and arm the dreamers to demand the impossible. We have sold millions of copies of our books, most often one at a time, face to face. We're old enough to know what we're doing and young enough to know what's at stake. Join us to create a better world.

PM Press
PO Box 23912
Oakland, CA 94623
www.pmpress.org

PM Press in Europe
europe@pmpress.org
www.pmpress.org.uk

FRIENDS OF PM PRESS

These are indisputably momentous times—the financial system is melting down globally and the Empire is stumbling. Now more than ever there is a vital need for radical ideas.

In the many years since its founding—and on a mere shoestring—PM Press has risen to the formidable challenge of publishing and distributing knowledge and entertainment for the struggles ahead. With hundreds of releases to date, we have published an impressive and stimulating array of literature, art, music, politics, and culture. Using every available medium, we've succeeded in connecting those hungry for ideas and information to those putting them into practice.

Friends of PM allows you to directly help impact, amplify, and revitalize the discourse and actions of radical writers, filmmakers, and artists. It provides us with a stable foundation from which we can build upon our early successes and provides a much-needed subsidy for the materials that can't necessarily pay their own way. You can help make that happen—and receive every new title automatically delivered to your door once a month—by joining as a Friend of PM Press. And, we'll throw in a free T-shirt when you sign up.

Here are your options:

- **$30 a month** Get all books and pamphlets plus 50% discount on all webstore purchases

- **$40 a month** Get all PM Press releases (including CDs and DVDs) plus 50% discount on all webstore purchases

- **$100 a month** Superstar—Everything plus PM merchandise, free downloads, and 50% discount on all webstore purchases

For those who can't afford $30 or more a month, we have **Sustainer Rates** at $15, $10, and $5. Sustainers get a free PM Press T-shirt and a 50% discount on all purchases from our website.

Your Visa or Mastercard will be billed once a month, until you tell us to stop. Or until our efforts succeed in bringing the revolution around. Or the financial meltdown of Capital makes plastic redundant. Whichever comes first.

Paths toward Utopia: Graphic Explorations of Everyday Anarchism

Cindy Milstein and Erik Ruin
with an Introduction by Josh MacPhee

ISBN: 978-1-60486-502-8
$14.95   120 pages

Consisting of ten collaborative picture-essays that weave Cindy Milstein's poetic words within Erik Ruin's intricate yet bold paper-cut and scratch-board images, *Paths toward Utopia* suggests some of the here-and-now practices that prefigure, however imperfectly, the self-organization that would be commonplace in an egalitarian society. The book mines what we do in our daily lives for the already-existent gems of a freer future—premised on anarchistic ethics like cooperation and direct democracy. Its pages depict everything from seemingly ordinary activities like using parks as our commons to grandiose occupations of public space that construct do-it-ourselves communities, if only temporarily, including pieces such as "The Gift," "Borrowing from the Library," "Solidarity Is a Pizza," and "Waking to Revolution." The aim is to supply hints of what it routinely would be like to live, every day, in a world created from below, where coercion and hierarchy are largely vestiges of the past.

Paths toward Utopia is not a rosy-eyed stroll, though. The book retains the tensions in present-day attempts to "model" horizontal institutions and relationships of mutual aid under increasingly vertical, exploitative, and alienated conditions. It tries to walk the line between potholes and potential. Yet if anarchist and other autonomist efforts are to serve as a clarion call to action, they must illuminate how people qualitatively, consensually, and ecologically shape their needs as well as desires. They must offer stepping-stones toward emancipation. This can only happen through experimentation, by us all, with diverse forms of self-determination and self-governance, even if riddled with contradictions in this contemporary moment. As the title piece to this book steadfastly asserts, "The precarious passage itself is our road map to a liberatory society."

"Writing-speaking differently is part of the struggle for the world we want to create and are creating, a world that moves against-and-beyond capitalism. These picture-essay-poems break the existing world both in what they say and how they say it. A fabulous book."
—John Holloway, author of *Crack Capitalism*

"Paths toward Utopia combines beautiful art, crafted insights, and exemplary stories to plant inspiring seeds of a better future. What more could one ask for?"
—Michael Albert, author of *Parecon: Life after Capitalism*

Mutual Aid: An Illuminated Factor of Evolution

Peter Kropotkin
Illustrated by N.O. Bonzo with an
Introduction by David Graeber & Andrej
Grubačić, Foreword by Ruth Kinna,
Postscript by GATS, and an Afterword
by Allan Antliff

ISBN: 978-1-62963-874-4 (paperback)
978-1-62963-875-1 (hardcover)
$30.00/$59.95   336 pages

One hundred years after his death, Peter Kropotkin is still one of the most inspirational figures of the anarchist movement. It is often forgotten that Kropotkin was also a world-renowned geographer whose seminal critique of the hypothesis of competition promoted by social Darwinism helped revolutionize modern evolutionary theory. An admirer of Darwin, he used his observations of life in Siberia as the basis for his 1902 collection of essays *Mutual Aid: A Factor of Evolution*. Kropotkin demonstrated that mutually beneficial cooperation and reciprocity—in both individuals and as a species—plays a far more important role in the animal kingdom and human societies than does individualized competitive struggle. Kropotkin carefully crafted his theory making the science accessible. His account of nature rejected Rousseau's romantic depictions and ethical socialist ideas that cooperation was motivated by the notion of "universal love." His understanding of the dynamics of social evolution shows us the power of cooperation—whether it is bison defending themselves against a predator or workers unionizing against their boss. His message is clear: solidarity is strength!

Every page of this new edition of *Mutual Aid* has been beautifully illustrated by one of anarchism's most celebrated current artists, N.O. Bonzo. The reader will also enjoy original artwork by GATS and insightful commentary by David Graeber, Ruth Kinna, Andrej Grubačić, and Allan Antliff.

"N.O. Bonzo has created a rare document, updating Kropotkin's anarchist classic
Mutual Aid, *by intertwining compelling imagery with an updated text. Filled with illustrious examples, their art gives the words and histories, past and present, resonance for new generations to seed flowers of cooperation to push through the concrete of resistance to show liberatory possibilities for collective futures."*
—scott crow, author of *Black Flags and Windmills* and *Setting Sights*

"Taking aim at both social Darwinists and Romantic dreamers, Kropotkin's classic text makes plain that the promise of liberation arises from our collective instinct to cooperate. In this new edition, lovingly illuminated by N.O. Bonzo, we can see the powerful amplifying effect of mutual aid firsthand."
—AK Thompson, author of *Black Bloc, White Riot*

For All the People: Uncovering the Hidden History of Cooperation, Cooperative Movements, and Communalism in America, 2nd Edition

John Curl with an Introduction by Ishmael Reed

ISBN: 978-1-60486-582-0
$29.95   608 pages

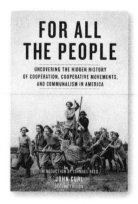

Seeking to reclaim a history that has remained largely ignored by most historians, this dramatic and stirring account examines each of the definitive American cooperative movements for social change—farmer, union, consumer, and communalist—that have been all but erased from collective memory. Focusing far beyond one particular era, organization, leader, or form of cooperation, *For All the People* documents the multigenerational struggle of the American working people for social justice. While the economic system was in its formative years, generation after generation of American working people challenged it by organizing visionary social movements aimed at liberating themselves from what they called wage slavery. Workers substituted a system based on cooperative work and constructed parallel institutions that would supersede the institutions of the wage system.

With an expansive sweep and breathtaking detail, this scholarly yet eminently readable chronicle follows the American worker from the colonial workshop to the modern mass-assembly line, from the family farm to the corporate hierarchy, ultimately painting a vivid panorama of those who built the United States and those who will shape its future.

This second edition contains a new introduction by Ishmael Reed; a new author's preface discussing cooperatives in the Great Recession of 2008 and their future in the 21st century; and a new chapter on the role co-ops played in the Food Revolution of the 1970s.

"It is indeed inspiring, in the face of all the misguided praise of 'the market', to be reminded by John Curl's new book of the noble history of cooperative work in the United States."
—Howard Zinn, author of *A People's History of the United States*

"John Curl's book For All the People *is a one-of-a-kind gem. He has done what no one else has by exploring the various permutations of 'cooperation' as a value system and as a movement throughout American history. He also makes clear that the cooperative alternative to wage-labor and exploitation still offers hope to those of us who want to see democracy permeate the world of work."*
—Steve Leikin, author of *The Practical Utopians: American Workers and the Cooperative Movement in the Gilded Age*

Other Avenues Are Possible: Legacy of the People's Food System of the San Francisco Bay Area

Shanta Nimbark Sacharoff

ISBN: 978-1-62963-232-2
$14.95   200 pages

Other Avenues Are Possible offers a vivid account of the dramatic rise and fall of the San Francisco People's Food System of the 1970s.

Weaving new interviews, historical research, and the author's personal story as a longstanding co-op member, the book captures the excitement of a growing radical social movement along with the struggles, heartbreaking defeats, and eventual resurgence of today's thriving network of Bay Area cooperatives, the greatest concentration of co-ops anywhere in the country.

Integral to the early natural foods movement, with a radical vision of "Food for People, Not for Profit," the People's Food System challenged agribusiness and supermarkets, and quickly grew into a powerful local network with nationwide influence before flaming out, often in dramatic fashion. *Other Avenues Are Possible* documents how food co-ops sprouted from grassroots organizations with a growing political awareness of global environmental dilapidation and unequal distribution of healthy foods to proactively serve their local communities. The book explores both the surviving businesses and a new network of support organizations that is currently expanding.

"In this book, Shanta Nimbark Sacharoff inspires us all by recounting how cooperation created other avenues for workers and consumers by developing a food system that not only promoted healthy food but wove within it practices that respect workers and the environment."
—E. Kim Coontz, executive director, California Center for Cooperative Development

"I have been waiting more than twenty years for this book! Shanta Nimbark Sacharoff's Other Avenues Are Possible *details the history of the People's Food System, a grand experiment in combining good food and workplace democracy.* Other Avenues *answers many of my questions about how the food politics of the Bay Area developed and points the way towards a better—and more cooperative—future. A must-read for anyone who eats food."*
—Gordon Edgar, author of *Cheesemonger: A Life on the Wedge* and a worker owner of Rainbow Grocery Cooperative

Towards Collective Liberation: Anti-Racist Organizing, Feminist Praxis, and Movement Building Strategy

Chris Crass with an Introduction by Chris Dixon and Foreword by Roxanne Dunbar-Ortiz

ISBN: 978-1-60486-654-4
$20.00   320 pages

Towards Collective Liberation: Anti-Racist Organizing, Feminist Praxis, and Movement Building Strategy is for activists engaging with dynamic questions of how to create and support effective movements for visionary systemic change. Chris Crass's collection of essays and interviews presents us with powerful lessons for transformative organizing through offering a firsthand look at the challenges and the opportunities of anti-racist work in white communities, feminist work with men, and bringing women of color feminism into the heart of social movements. Drawing on two decades of personal activist experience and case studies of anti-racist social justice organizations, Crass insightfully explores ways of transforming divisions of race, class, and gender into catalysts for powerful vision, strategy, and movement building in the United States today.

"*In his writing and organizing, Chris Crass has been at the forefront of building the grassroots, multi-racial, feminist movements for justice we need.* Towards Collective Liberation *takes on questions of leadership, building democratic organizations, and movement strategy, on a very personal level that invites us all to experiment and practice the way we live our values while struggling for systemic change.*"
—Elizabeth 'Betita' Martinez, founder of the Institute for Multiracial Justice and author of *De Colores Means All of Us: Latina Views for a Multi-Colored Century*

"*Chris Crass goes into the grassroots to produce a political vision that will catalyze political change. These are words from the heart, overflowing onto the streets.*"
—Vijay Prashad, author of *Darker Nations: A People's History of the Third World*

"*A deeply important, engaged, and learned defense of anarchism, class politics, and anti-racism. Grounded in study, organizing, and struggle,* Towards Collective Liberation *is a significant contribution to the recent history of the U.S. left.*"
—David Roediger, author of *Wages of Whiteness*

Black Flags and Windmills: Hope, Anarchy, and the Common Ground Collective

scott crow with Forewords by Kathleen Cleaver and John P. Clark

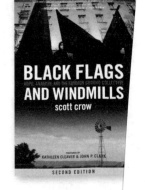

ISBN: 978-1-60486-453-3
$20.00   288 pages

When both levees and governments failed in New Orleans after Hurricane Katrina, the anarchist-inspired Common Ground Collective was created to fill the void. With the motto of "Solidarity Not Charity," they worked to create power from below—building autonomous projects, programs, and spaces of self-sufficiency like health clinics and neighborhood assemblies, while also supporting communities defending themselves from white militias and police brutality, illegal home demolitions, and evictions.

Black Flags and Windmills—equal parts memoir, history, and organizing philosophy vividly intertwines Common Ground cofounder scott crow's experiences and ideas with Katrina's reality, illustrating how people can build local grassroots power for collective liberation. It is a story of resisting indifference, rebuilding hope amid collapse, and struggling against the grain to create better worlds.

The expanded second edition includes up-to-date interviews and discussions between crow and some of today's most articulate and influential activists and organizers on topics ranging from grassroots disaster relief efforts (both economic and environmental); dealing with infiltration, interrogation, and surveillance from the State; and a new photo section that vividly portrays scott's experiences as anarchist, activist, and movement organizer in today's world.

"*scott crow's trenchant memoir of grassroots organizing is an important contribution a history of movements that far too often goes untold.*"
—Amy Goodman, host and executive producer of *Democracy Now!*

"*This revised and expanded edition weaves scott crow's frontline experiences with resilient, honest discussion of grassroots political movement-building.*"
—Will Potter, author of *Green Is the New Red: An Insider's Account of a Social Movement Under Siege*

"*It is a brilliant, detailed, and humble book written with total frankness and at the same time a revolutionary poet's passion. It makes the reader feel that we too, with our emergency heart as our guide, can do anything; we only need to begin.*"
—Marina Sitrin, author of *Horizontalism: Voices of Popular Power in Argentina*